Praise for *The Girl in the Red Boots*

"This is an introspective work . . . a fascinating examination of how daughters make peace with their moms."
—*Kirkus Reviews*

"In this engaging book, Rabinor reflects on the most complex, intense and important of all relationships, the one between mothers and daughters. She shares the story of her journey from pain and anger to acceptance and gratitude and explores the journeys of other mothers and daughters, too. Rabinor's professional work with eating disorders has given her a unique vantage point on these most timeless of stories. Her book is candid, fresh and inspiring."
—Mary Pipher, author of *Women Rowing North* and *Reviving Ophelia*

"A riveting read that reminds us that parenting is fragile, love is always flawed and it's never too late to understand ourselves and our mothers."
—Jane Goldberg, author of *The Dark Side of Love*

"Dr. Rabinor cuts through the common misunderstandings of therapy in an intimate sharing; she meets her patients pain for pain. Reading the insights of this wounded healer about the lingering effects of childhood trauma, I nodded in agreement, dazzled."
—Jesse Kornbluth, author and screenwriter

"I applaud Judy Rabinor for giving women permission to examine their mother-daughter relationships. She shows us it's never too late to heal our childhood wounds."
—June Alexander, PhD, author of *A Collaborative Approach to Eating Disorders*

"In this captivating book, Dr. Rabinor lifts the therapeutic veil, gently guiding the reader to discover what happens when one expresses pent-up love rather than pent-up anger. Immersing myself in *The Girl in the Red Boots* felt like entering a secret sorority resulting in an enhanced appreciation and longing for my own mother. This is a must-read for anyone who has or is a mother!"
—Dr. Amy Banks, coauthor of *Wired to Connect: The Surprising Link Between Brain Science and Strong, Healthy Relationships*

"*The Girl with the Red Boots* is a treasure. Judy Rabinor is a gifted storyteller, an expert clinician and a wise woman. This is a book that sings with personal growth, cross-generational love, and contagious hope."
—Michael P. Levine, PhD, author and Professor Emeritus, Kenyon College

"Read this book slowly. Your own mother will seep into the pages . . . and you will want to push her away. Judy's story helps us look deeply at our own mothers, to see what we may have missed, to quiet our anger. She helps us start to forgive. A compelling story not just about the author but also about you."
—Judith Brisman, PhD, author of *Surviving an Eating Disorder: Strategies for Family and Friends*

"*The Girl in the Red Boots* is delicious. This book is about personal growth over a lifetime. It's about healing as a never-ending process. It's about the fallacy that good therapy requires people to express their anger and disappointment to heal. A feast for the heart and soul, and a must read for all."
—Margo Maine, PhD, author of *Pursuing Perfection: Eating Disorders, Body Myths, and Women at Midlife and Beyond*, (with Joe Kelly) and *Father Hunger*

"*The Girl in the Red Boots* is a deep and beautiful memoir. Judy Rabinor draws you into your inner world as she explores love and healing in her relationship with her mother. A must-read!"
—Judi Goldstein, MSS, LSW, vice president of The Renfrew Center Foundation

"Judith Rabinor proves Socrates right when he said "an unexamined life is not worth living." Switching roles, from therapist to client, Dr. Rabinor mines her own complicated relationship with her mother to show that memories that might seem trivial are actually essential in understanding what drives us."
—Charles Salzberg, author of *Second Story Man*, award-winning novelist and journalist

"Unlike memoirs of cataclysmic abuse, Judy's story is sure to resonate with the stress and distress of your own life."
—Sondra Kronberg, MS, Founder, *Chats in the Living Room at EDTC/FEED*

"A compelling, deeply personal book about the complexities of the mother-daughter relationship. A gifted storyteller, Judith Rabinor skillfully reveals the healing power of story."
—Anita Johnston, PhD, author, *Eating in the Light of the Moon: How Women Can Transform Their Relationships with Food Through Myths, Metaphors, and Storytelling*

"Impeccable storytelling makes for a riveting journey. The memoir provides a beautiful mode for holding seemingly contradictory feelings about loved ones; her compassionate authenticity normalizes and celebrates this reality of the human experience."
—Katie Rickel, PhD, CEO of Structure House

The
Girl
IN THE
Red Boots

The
Girl
IN THE
Red Boots

Making Peace
with My Mother

JUDITH RUSKAY RABINOR, PhD

She Writes Press

Published 2021
Printed in the United States of America
Print ISBN: 978-1-64742-040-6
E-ISBN: 978-1-64742-041-3
Library of Congress Control Number: 2020922177

For information, address:
She Writes Press
1569 Solano Ave #546
Berkeley, CA 94707

Interior design by Tabitha Lahr

She Writes Press is a division of SparkPoint Studio, LLC.

In memory of my parents, my first and most important teachers:

my mother, Peggy
(1918-2011)

and

my father, Everett
(1917-1972)

"Every mother contains her daughter in herself and every daughter her mother and every mother extends backwards into her mother and forwards into her daughter."

—CARL G. JUNG, MD

"We are taught to believe that pent-up hostility is dangerous, yet the real tragedy is pent-up love. . . . The release of pent-up love and respect for our mothers brings the added gift of love and respect for ourselves."

—PAULA J. CAPLAN, PhD

Contents

PART SEVEN: Waiting

PART EIGHT: Retelling Our Stories

Prologue

On the windowsill in my psychotherapy office sits a sand-art picture, a simple black frame filled with colored sand. Each time you shake the frame, the sand shifts seamlessly into a new design.

I keep it there for my patients. When they notice it, I ask them if they'd like to examine it. "Shake it," I suggest. Then I tell them why I keep it in my office.

"Our minds are like sand dunes, filled with hidden treasures, your stories," I say. "Every story you have ever lived or imagined is buried inside you, waiting to be revealed as the grains of sand shift and open up new possibilities."

All of us are storytellers. We don't know when we might unexpectedly shake up a forgotten story, just like shaking the sand-art picture brings up new images. Reality—like our stories—is always shifting and deepening, which is the goal of therapy: to awaken stories that remind us of our vulnerabilities, strengths, and new possibilities.

I don't tell my patients my own story, but it's my story about my mother that has informed my thinking.

As I write this, it's been almost eight years since my mother died at ninety-three, but I still sometimes find myself arguing with her in my mind, alternately judging and forgiving her, rethinking our complicated bond. It is said that many people who become psychotherapists do so to better understand themselves. This is certainly true for me. Over the past forty years, I've specialized in the mother-daughter relationship. Helping my patients understand their mothers has helped me become familiar with parts of myself—and my mother—I might never have known if not for the stories I've heard.

Stories are great teachers; they have the power to heal. The tales from my office and my life may help you untangle your stuck places and develop compassion for yourself and, possibly, for your mother. While you didn't pick your mother, as an adult you always have the opportunity to choose new pathways. It's never too late to let go of frustrated expectations and celebrate a connection you might have thought was doomed to disappointment and hurt.

PART ONE:

Welcome to Womanhood

Imagine that you are searching through a box of old photographs, seeking a picture of your mother. Find one that strikes you, and look at it closely. Notice the expression on your mother's face. What is she wearing? Notice her clothing. What is the background of this picture? If it is outdoors, what is the weather like? The light? If it is indoors, notice the furnishings that catch your eye. If there are other people in the picture, how is your mother relating to them? As you contemplate her at this particular moment in her life, be aware of what she is feeling.

The Most Important Woman
You Have Ever Known

It's 1991 and I'm elated, seated in a small circle in the center of a crowded conference room with six volunteers. My workshop, Therapists as Wounded Healers: Healing the Mother-Daughter Relationship, is packed. I'm at the prestigious National Eating Disorders Organization's conference in Columbus, Ohio, training mental health professionals on how to work with daughters with eating disorders and their mothers. It's a diverse group; mostly women dressed in every imaginable outfit, from conservative business attire to colorful, flowing bohemian garb, fill the room, all eager to learn about treating the families of clients with eating disorders.

I created this workshop to help therapists pay attention to their inner lives; therapists' wounds need to be honored, rather than buried. When we work with families, our own wounds are inevitably triggered, which is why many therapists shy away from working with families. Therapists need to notice and become comfortable with how easy it is to blame, demonize, or idealize one's mother. Working on ourselves is the therapist's best tool when it comes to maintaining objectivity with patients.

3

Earlier, I had asked participants to imagine rummaging through a box of old pictures. "Find a photograph of your mother," I instructed, in a slow, quiet voice. "Take your time, and select an image that has something special to tell you about who she is as a person." I paused and lowered my voice. "Your mother is the most important woman you will ever know." Pause. "Your mother welcomed you to womanhood." I chose my language carefully, intentionally creating an atmosphere of reverence and respect for mothering and motherhood, both of which the culture at large generally devalues.

Now, all eyes are on me, awaiting further direction.

"We're going to introduce ourselves to one another, this time in a special way. Bring up the picture of your mother that came up for you in our meditation. This is *one* of the internal pictures you carry of your mother. Your mother." I deliberately emphasize the word "one" to underscore the complexity of the mother-daughter bond, and I repeat "your mother" to highlight the uniqueness of the relationship. "When it comes to our mothers, people generally have mixed feelings." Since the beginning of the workshop, I have emphasized that ambivalence is part of all healthy, close relationships.

"Just follow my lead," I add. "I'm Judy, daughter of Peggy. I was welcomed to the world of womanhood by Peggy, captain of the cheerleaders, always smiling."

As I speak, my heart begins to race and my head pounds. My prepared words feel hollow. At this moment, I have no access to the picture I usually bring up, the mother I romanticized throughout childhood: the pretty, popular captain of the cheerleading squad who married her high school boyfriend, the captain of the football team, my dad. At this moment, it is my neglectful, unreachable mother who creeps into my mind. I freeze at the traumatic memory that arises.

It was a hot June day, and I was eight years old, lying in a hospital bed, sweating. I had been weeping, and my eyes were glued shut with my tears. I needed my mommy, and she was not here. I cracked my eyes open to see if she'd arrived. She hadn't.

I gazed around the stark, stuffy room. I kept staring at my new pink silk party blouse hanging in the metal closet in the corner. My lace-trimmed white cotton socks peeked out of my black patent-leather Mary Jane shoes on the floor. I wanted to scream, but I couldn't because my throat was raw and burning. A white uniform was speaking. "It's all over, dearie. You're back in your room."

My room? Like a magician, she read my mind.

"You probably don't remember coming up here last night, or me, either. I'm your nurse."

Nurse? I know only one nurse, Miss Elaine, who works in my doctor's cozy office around the corner from my house.

"You were drugged when they brought you in from the operating room last night, and I'm taking care of you. Don't cry—your mother will be here soon; visiting hours start at noon. I know your throat is sore, honey—that's what happens when they take out the tonsils. But you'll feel better—I'm sure she'll bring your favorite ice cream. The cold will really feel good on your throat. So wipe away your tears."

I had been dressed for my cousin Winnie's birthday party. Instead, my mother had brought me to the hospital. My head throbbed as I remembered the sinking feeling I had when the orderly tore me away from her. A tear trickled down my face.

"Wipe away your tears; you're going to be fine!" said the white uniform. But I wasn't fine. For my whole life, my mother had told me I was fine, even when I wasn't.

It would be more than a decade before I confronted my mother. "You should have warned me I was having my tonsils out, Ma. You should have prepared me. Why didn't you tell me the truth?"

I am suddenly jolted back to the present moment. I'm leading a workshop, and I'm overwhelmed by my own dark feelings. A familiar ache runs through me; I thought I'd resolved my resentments about my mother, but I am wrong. I'm terrified and flustered. I've attempted to create a climate in this workshop that validates the complexity and ambivalence inherent in all intimate relationships, especially the mother-daughter bond. I've framed this workshop as an opportunity for everyone to work on the unhealed parts of themselves. At forty-nine years old, I have a professional reputation that rests upon being an authentic, vulnerable, and self-revealing psychotherapist. "Without hard work on ourselves, we are doomed to repeat the past" is one of my signature statements, yet now I must face it—an unhealed wound has derailed me. I'm having trouble staying present and centered.

The group is waiting for me to begin. Knowing I need to pull myself together, I whisper my mantra and ground myself: "Breathe in deeply, and exhale completely." As I take three deep breaths, slowly inhaling and exhaling, I feel my body calm down and I regain my equilibrium. I am re-anchored in the present moment.

A quick glance around the circle, and I realize the group is oblivious to the fact that I drifted off. The introductory process I've activated has been mobilized. The woman to my right, with long, curly, salt-and-pepper hair, is speaking. Her voice is a whisper, barely audible. I've missed her name and must lean forward to hear her.

"Speak up, and repeat yourself, please," I say gently, wondering if she is always so timid.

"I'm Rhonda, daughter of Mary Beth. I was welcomed to the world of womanhood by Mary Beth, always . . ." Her voice disappears. Rhonda is wincing. A low mumble has replaced her whisper. "I was welcomed by my mother, Mary Beth, always depressed." Her eyes are downcast. Like so many daughters of depressed mothers, Rhonda cannot find her voice. "Like mother, like daughter" is one of the themes that has come up all morning as the group participants have worked on understanding, repairing, and deepening their relationships with their mothers.

Next to Rhonda sits a young woman who looks to be barely out of high school. Tossing her short hair back and thrusting her face forward, she speaks in an unusually loud voice.

"I'm Marilyn, daughter of Sophia." She stops speaking and smiles at the group. "I was welcomed to the world of womanhood by Sophia, the sexpot."

What is it like to have a sexpot for a mother? I wonder. A picture of my own flirtatious mother jumps into my mind. She is wearing a navy blue taffeta dress. She loved to dance in a sexy manner—another of her legacies to me. I bookmark Sophia's introduction; later, I will invite the group to explore how a daughter's sexuality is shaped in the family she grows up in.

Introductions flow. "I'm Julie, daughter of Gloria, I was welcomed to the world of womanhood by Gloria, queen of secrets." The speaker is a slight woman in her forties whose voice sounds like chimes. She is followed by Maxine, a stocky, thirtysomething woman with blonde hair, who was welcomed to womanhood by Karina, always at the stove.

The last to speak in our small inner circle is a slight, anxious-sounding, middle-aged woman with flame-red hair. "I'm LuAnne, and I was welcomed to womanhood by JoAnne, large and always smiling."

What did LuAnne's mother do with her anger? I wonder. *Hide it beneath a smile, like my mother did?* LuAnne described her mother as large. Like many mothers of daughters with eating disorders, did JoAnne bury her intolerable feelings beneath binges?

While one part of my brain has refocused on the group, another part of me wants to disappear. I'm feeling like a fraud. Here I am, a psychologist, training professionals to revisit and repair their own ruptures with their mothers while my own unhealed wounds prevent me from doing the essence of what I'm teaching: honoring our mothers. I'm mired in shame. How will I be able to help others if my scars are so raw? What do I need to do to heal my own ancient wounds?

Just Fine

"You'll be fine!" My mother beamed as she placed a bowl of chocolate ice cream on my tray. We were home from the hospital, and my throat burned so much, I felt scared to eat. Even drinking small sips left me terrified I'd drown. Afraid I'd suffocate or choke, I dreaded sleeping. Somehow, I got through those first, long days. Eventually, my grandmother Sophie came over with a copy of the latest Nancy Drew book, *The Mystery of the Black Keys*. By the end of that summer, I'd read every book in the Nancy Drew series, twice. I told no one how I felt.

"You'll be fine! Everything will work out—you'll see." From the time I was a small girl, this was my mother's pat response to everything. It didn't matter if I was crying because I'd fallen off my bike while whizzing down the steep hill at the end of our Long Island street or, when I was older, because the queen bee of the mean girls in my seventh-grade class had shunned me. No matter what, my mother's reaction was always predictable: "Don't let this bother you, honey," or "It hurts now, but you'll get over it." I never felt as if she took the time to stand in my shoes, listen carefully, and feel for or with me. Later, I would identify what I yearned for. The missing ingredient was my mother's genuine empathic presence.

From a skinned knee to a broken heart, the solution to most dilemmas was a hug, a glass of milk, and two chocolate chip cookies. The cheerleading captain always wore boots with pom-poms and carried a shiny baton! But never did she really listen to me when I was anxious, worried, or upset. She always dismissed my feelings.

By the time I was a teenager, my mother's uber optimism and enthusiasm had transformed, replacing the glass of milk and two cookies with Loehmann's shopping expeditions. At my mother's side, I became a skilled bargain hunter. Later, when my father's business improved, we shopped sales at upscale department stores like Lord & Taylor and Blooming-dale's. Shopping, according to my mom, was a quick fix for anything that might ail you, including and especially, death, divorce, and depression. What I learned as a child, literally and figuratively, was to soothe myself through retail therapy and to always get back on my bike.

It wasn't until I was twenty-two years old and began psy-chotherapy that I revisited my tonsillectomy. I began therapy after a boyfriend dumped me unexpectedly and I found myself unable to get out of bed. I had no idea that this abandonment had triggered my tonsils trauma. Later on, when I became a psychologist, I would appreciate that deeply disturbing expe-riences are overwhelming and can leave lasting scars. But as a twenty-two-year-old, I knew only that I was devastated by the loss of this boyfriend.

Fortunately, I wound up in the office of Dr. Earl Saxe, a gentle, soft-spoken man who introduced me to the joy of being carefully listened to. Instead of responding to me with optimistic platitudes and quick fixes, he introduced me to a way of being that changed my life. He asked me to slow down, stay with my feelings, and take them seriously, instead of burying them or running away. His careful, quiet presence offered me a cocoon-like second home. An eager learner, I quickly understood that present problems are often rooted in the past. Within two months, I began a psychoanalysis, which would last several years.

Feeling seen, known, and held in my analyst's heart was a profound and novel experience. For the most part, Dr. Saxe was a silent, steady listener, but his memory for what seemed like the tiniest details about my life amazed me. To my naive mind, he seemed to have an astounding knack for asking simple but profound questions that introduced me to the power of emotional archeological excavation. As we dug into the soil of my childhood, it didn't take long before I stumbled upon an underground river of unhealed wounds that, unbeknownst to me, continued to fester.

In this initial, dredging-up-the-past phase of therapy, certain moments remain etched in my memory. Dr. Saxe's expression was aghast when I told him about my confusion upon waking in the hospital room and about my focus on my pink party blouse with the shiny pearl buttons lying on the floor of the metal closet. I thought I heard a low gasp and a crack in his voice as I shared the story about my cousin's birthday party.

My Cousin Winnie's
Birthday Party

"Whatcha doing, homework?" my mom asked cheerfully, sticking her head into my room minutes after I'd returned from school.

"Nancy Drew time," I said—shorthand for, "Don't bother me; I'm busy." Lounging on my bed, I was engrossed in the latest addition to my ever-growing Nancy Drew mystery series.

"My Judy is probably the only girl in third grade who has read all those books—yes, every book in the series, some twice!" my mother liked to say. I was one of the best readers in my class—my mother loved to throw that in as well.

"Now," she said, "keep me company while I make dinner, hon. Come on down; bring your homework, and I'll make a pitcher of lemonade."

The lemonade sealed the deal. My next-door neighbor Linda's mom made the best lemonade, with tons of sugar, and I was hoping my mom's would be just as syrupy sweet.

So there I sat with my homework at the kitchen table, drinking iced lemonade from my favorite glass, the one my mother usually saved for special occasions. It was the lone survivor of a set of six pale blue iced-tea glasses, a wedding gift from Uncle Ben, my dad's boss when they lived in Maryland. Like my forehead, the delicate crystal was covered with bands of tiny sweat beads on this late-June afternoon, hot and muggy on Long Island. The following day would be the last day of school for two months.

"I just want to remind you that I'll be picking you up right after school tomorrow," Mom said, as she finished molding chopped meat into four perfectly rounded quarter-pound hamburgers, our standard Monday dinner. Maybe I looked surprised, because I remember her adding, "No piano lesson tomorrow, remember? It's Winnie's birthday party. Let's go upstairs and lay out your party outfit so it will be ready."

There she was at two forty-five the next day, waiting for me at the schoolyard gate. Within minutes, I was back home, changing into my special clothes: a pink satin blouse and a gray felt skirt. The soft satin was trimmed with gray ribbing on the collar, and small, elegant gray pearl buttons ran neatly down the front. But the centerpiece was the gray felt skirt with a huge French poodle, stitched with the words "Love Me, Love My Dog" in red wool on the front.

Within minutes, I was sitting next to my mother in the passenger seat of our new Buick convertible. The top was down, and we were drenched in sunlight, off to Winnie's birthday party. My mom's long brown hair was piled on top of her head in the fancy coif she saved only for special occasions, and I was busily arranging my precious skirt so that I could gaze easily into Frankie's big black poodle eyes embroidered in fluffy black angora on the front.

It's hard to know what really happened next. All I remember is that I was suddenly in a small room with faded walls. My mother and I were seated on a hard wooden bench that reminded me of the benches outside the principal's office at my school. The only thing to look at from where I sat was a huge cross with Jesus nailed to it, which took up most of the faded yellow wall. Two nuns were busy reading names from a long list, calling people to their scraped-up wooden desk, which matched the bench, and handing out and collecting papers. I was shivering; being Jewish, I had never been up close to a nun and in fact was afraid of them. I had heard from my neighbor Timmy that nuns could be really brutal.

"Ma, where are we?" I asked. "Why are we—Jews—here in a room with a huge cross?"

She probably smiled and squeezed my hand and I quieted down, until we were no longer in the place with the cross on the faded yellow wall and had been ushered into a small, dim room with no windows. A fan hummed, and wisps from my mother's hair blew around her face. Now, a red blazer with wispy hair like my mom's was asking questions, and my mom answered: date of birth, address . . . I zoned out.

"Judy, I'll come visit you tomorrow—after the operation."

I tuned back in. *Visit me tomorrow? What is she talking about?*

"Aren't we going to Winnie's birthday party, Ma?"

A woman in a white uniform grasped my hand firmly and led me down the hall. I screamed as the smile on my mom's face got smaller and smaller. Just as it was about to disappear, she repeated, "I'll see you tomorrow, honey, after the operation is over. You'll be feeling fine by then. And no whining, Judy."

The woman walked me gently through a series of swinging doors, each one separating me from my mom. The white uniform was talking. "Having your tonsils out is very routine, nothing to worry about. Yes, it will hurt a little, but the best part is that you'll get to eat all the ice cream you can ever imagine. Can you tell me your favorite flavor?"

I was crying too hard to answer.

"I bet you like chocolate."

Please Ma, come back now.

"Your mother will be here tomorrow, after the operation is done, and I'll tell her to bring chocolate ice cream. It will help your throat feel cool, not so raw!"

"Come back nooooooooooooow!" Strapped down on a stretcher, I felt a blackness fall around me as I was wheeled through a series of swinging doors and the suffocating smell of ether closed in.

I opened my eyes to a blur. *Is this the same or a different nurse telling me the operation is over?* The poodle on my skirt gazed at me with a comforting smile from the metal closet in the corner of my hospital room.

Although it had been fifteen years since my tonsillectomy, by the time I finished telling Dr. Saxe my story, I was sobbing. Thinking I heard him sniffle, I sat up on the couch and turned around; for a moment, I could have sworn his eyes were filled with tears. This surprised me, since I had been reading avidly about psychoanalysis and had learned that analysts are supposed to keep their feelings to themselves and maintain a "blank screen." Fifty years ago, even subtle disclosures by analysts were frowned upon, considered taboo and even dangerous. Nor were analysts meant to give direct suggestions to patients. Instead, they were supposed to listen quietly in a way that would prompt the patient to be introspective, insightful and ultimately choose new behaviors.

I am still unclear whether my behavior was the result of Dr. Saxe's direct or indirect suggestion, but eventually I mustered my courage and confronted my mother. I'd gone back to my parents' home for the weekend, and she and I were sitting at the breakfast table on a sunny June morning.

"Why did you make up that story about Winnie's birthday party, Ma? Why didn't you tell me the truth, that I was having my tonsils out?"

My mother's response to my confrontation only unsettled me further. All I could eke out of her was that my pediatrician had advised her to spare me unnecessary worry. "What good would have come of knowing you were going to the hospital? You would have been a wreck for weeks!"

"Unnecessary worry? Are you crazy? Do you know how scared I was to wake up in the hospital alone?"

She shrugged and held her ground calmly. "I'm sorry, dear. I know you don't understand, but I did exactly what Dr. Steinman recommended—he thought there was no reason to make you nervous. I thought a little white lie would be okay, and I was trying to do my best."

This is how things were handled back then, I was told. Neither my mother nor I had any way of knowing how much pain this moment would cause me.

Little white lies, I learned, were harmless. I was growing up in a world where secrets and deception were a way of life. People had barely any awareness back then that white lies were not harmless and could create distrust and a fear of betrayal that might leave lifelong scars in its wake. Waking up alone in a scary hospital after a "surprise" surgery was enough to shock and overwhelm my nervous system. For most of my life, I was unaware that I was suffering from an unhealed trauma. It would take almost half a century for mental health professionals to understand the nature of and treatment for trauma.

Julie, Daughter of Gloria: Queen of Secrets

"**D**r. Rabinor, do you have a minute? I'm Julie Gilmore. It's okay if I call you Judy, right? After the work we did together yesterday, I feel like I actually know you."

It's the morning after the Healing the Mother-Daughter Relationship workshop, and I'm standing in the Marriott hotel lobby, waiting for an elevator. I'm eager to return to my room, pack, get to the airport, and go back home to my two children, when a tap on the shoulder stops me. A trim woman in a stylish pinstripe suit is smiling at me. Long auburn bangs and a neat pageboy frame her intense, dark eyes. A warm smile spreads across her face. I recognize her voice immediately—Julie was in my workshop yesterday and volunteered to work with me in front of the group. She had a particularly powerful experience in the workshop.

"Judy is fine, of course."

"I want to thank you for your workshop. I'm so grateful."

The word "grateful" stops me. I've presented this workshop several times, received many compliments, but "grateful"— this is a first. I feel my face flush. I've never been good at compliments.

"I'm so glad our paths crossed. I've been thinking about contacting you—how serendipitous to find you here." She lowers her voice. "Your workshop was incredibly profound for me. If you have a minute, I'd like to share with you what happened for me."

I nod. Even though I'm late, this is a request I can't deny.

"I came to your workshop because I'm a therapist who works with patients with eating disorders and their mothers, but really, I came because of my mother. We have a very difficult relationship. We stopped speaking last winter."

It's now October. I quickly do the math. Even though my mother unnerved me, I couldn't imagine cutting off contact for ten months.

"A story you told about one of your patients made me realize I'm still angry at my mother—and my anger imprisons me. I thought I'd gotten over my rage, but I realized I haven't, which was why I volunteered to work with you. I had a real breakthrough yesterday, and I want to thank you."

For a therapist, the word "breakthrough" is a conversation stopper. The majority of people, in life and in therapy, plod on, making small changes, one building upon another, with frequent slips. Even though therapy can be life changing, real breakthroughs occur only occasionally, generally after many months, if not years, of therapeutic work. And Julie Gilmore is not a patient but a workshop participant who is also a therapist, telling me she was transformed in my three-hour presentation. I wonder what occurred to move her so deeply.

"What happened?" I ask. "Any thoughts or ideas about exactly what went on for you?" I stop talking, hoping to leave space for her to sift through her thoughts, feelings, and memories.

Julie squints and wrinkles her forehead thoughtfully. I am hopeful that she will pinpoint whatever might have led to her moment of awakening. I am always interested in improving my workshops, but more important, I have a personal agenda.

Notwithstanding years of psychoanalysis and psychotherapy, I still can anguish over my connection to my unreachable mother. I know she loves me, but it is easy for me to feel neglected or obliterated by her. By now, I am aware that my desire to become a psychologist was motivated not only by the wish to help others heal, but also by a wish to heal myself and understand how my own family dynamics shaped my life.

"Right after your workshop, I went straight to my room and I called my mother," she replied. "We made a plan. I'll be visiting her for the Christmas holiday." Tears gathered in the corners of Julie's eyes.

"You called your mother?" I said. "To feel something shift is one thing, but to do something, to reach out and reconnect, that's a big deal." While many people think that having an emotional experience in a therapy session or a workshop is a breakthrough, these moments rarely lead to real and lasting change. But Julie had taken a huge step. She'd transformed an experience into an action. I wondered what exactly had impacted her. Perhaps her "breakthrough" held some wisdom for me—and others.

Julie shrugged. "I'm not sure what happened, but I'm moving to New York City next month and would love to set up a consultation with you. Do you have any time?"

I told her I'd check my calendar and get back to her. Just as I was about to say goodbye, she spoke up again.

"I just thought of something else that happened to me in the workshop. It was when I introduced myself and said, 'I'm Julie, daughter of Gloria. I was welcomed to the world of womanhood by Gloria, queen of secrets,' that I started to cry. Just saying those words was so powerful." She paused. "Maybe it's because 'queen of secrets' is so pejorative, but being 'welcomed to the world of womanhood' is such a loving image."

I nodded. Julie was reminding me of a common conundrum: Love is complicated and messy, often tinged with ambivalence containing dark feelings.

"Perhaps I began to soften when you introduced yourself. I remember you saying, 'I am Judy, daughter of Peggy, I was welcomed to womanhood by Peggy, captain of the cheerleaders, always smiling.'" Her eyes looked as if they were about to fill up again. "In my own way, as a clinical office manager, I'm also a captain of the cheerleaders." We both laughed. Just then, the elevator door opened. "I'll call you next week."

"Please do. I'll look forward to hearing from you," I said, stepping inside the elevator as the doors slid closed.

Back in my hotel room, I race to pack up and get organized. The clock is ticking. My two children are being dropped off at my house in Lido Beach, Long Island, at dinnertime by my ex-husband, who has given me a strict deadline. So far, our joint custody arrangement is working out smoothly, and I certainly don't want to miss my flight and antagonize him, yet I am compelled to hear more.

As I gather my scattered clothing and papers, Julie's face stays with me. "The queen of secrets"—the phrase hums evocatively. I am looking forward to hearing about her secretive mother and how Julie let go of her anger; I'm eager to understand how my workshop evoked such depth. I'm looking forward to getting on the plane and writing up my notes about what I learned anew—a mother's essence is passed on to the next generation. The words of my former graduate-school professor, Dr. Stan Kaplan, suddenly come to mind. I can see his shaggy gray hair and warm smile as he taught about the power of experiential work.

Tell me, I forget.
Show me, I may remember.
Involve me, I learn.

My mind flashes back to my work with Julie yesterday, in the final exercise of the workshop.

"Is there anyone who would like to work on what came up for you when you accessed the picture of your mother?" I asked the group.

Julie's hand shot up.

After thanking her for her courage to volunteer and be vulnerable, I placed two chairs in the middle of the room for us to sit facing each other. Then I let her know that if at any time she felt uncomfortable or uneasy, we would stop.

"Let's start over and reintroduce ourselves to one another," I suggested. "I'll begin. I'm Judy, daughter of Peggy. I was welcomed to the world of womanhood by Peggy, captain of the cheerleaders, always smiling."

After a pause, Julie spoke in a deep and husky voice. "I'm Julie, daughter of Gloria. I was welcomed to the world of womanhood by Gloria, queen of secrets." Her brown eyes were open wide.

"Go inside; take a moment to be with the queen of secrets," I said. "See the picture of your mother that you brought up in our exercise. See her, listen to her, and sense her. How old is she?"

Eyes closed, Julie remained silent. Her breathing was shallow.

"Take three deep breaths; inhale deeply; exhale completely," I said, and noticed her breaths deepen. "Now, allow the queen of secrets to come into focus and imagine you are telling her that you have learned about a secret she has kept from you. How do you tell her—how do you express yourself? Notice what she looks like as you tell her you know the secret she has kept from you. Is she listening to you? What does the expression on her face tell you? Allow the scene to unfold, and notice what feelings come up in your body. It's not necessary to tell us the secret, although you are welcome to do so. You can speak or remain silent—whatever is best for you. What's important is that you allow yourself to feel whatever it is you feel. Let whatever happens happen." My instructions were based on what I had learned over years of being a therapist, being a patient, and working on myself: Deep breathing is a pathway into emotional pain. To live a fulfilling life, it's necessary to face our demons. While our instinct is to run from emotional pain, only by staring it in the face and embracing it are we able to release it.

Within seconds, tears were rolling down Julie's cheeks.

"See if there are any words that go with your tears," I said. "You have the right to say as much or as little as you care to."

"How could you do this to me, Mom? Do you know what it was like to find out? To find out from neighbors what you couldn't tell me yourself? Why? Why couldn't you, Mom? Why couldn't you?" Julie's voice was shrill and rising.

"How old are you now?" I asked.

Julie was sobbing. "I am a teenager. Fourteen or fifteen."

"How does your mother react?"

"She's crying, too."

It was clear that Julie had accessed an old wound. In training workshops, I was generally careful to protect participants from revealing too much too soon. I wanted to guide Julie to deepen her feelings, but I knew revealing the content of her hurt with a group of strangers was unnecessary and could even be dangerous. It was her feelings, rather than the actual story, that I wanted to evoke.

"Tell your mother what's going on for you," I suggested. "Tell her how you feel."

By now, Julie was gasping between her sobs.

"See if there is something you want or need to say to your mother, Gloria, queen of secrets."

Julie began speaking softly. "Stop crying and listen to me, Mom. Listen to me!" Her voice grew louder as she began shrieking. "I will never trust you again, Mom. You are a liar." Her face scrunched up and turned beet red as she breathed rapidly. "How could you keep this secret from me? I had the right to know this, Mom!"

"Take another breath, deep into your heart, Julie," I said. "You may want to place your hand on your heart." Placing a hand on one's heart is a quick way to feel grounded and to self-regulate. "Take your time," I said. "Tell your mother whatever it is you need to say. How does she respond? Inhale deeply; exhale completely. Just allow yourself to notice what's going on inside."

As Julie placed her hand on her heart, her breathing quieted down. My voice seemed to have a soothing effect on her, too. Within moments, her sobs had ceased.

"And what's going on with you now?" I asked.

Tearfully, Julie smiled. "My mother heard me. She's crying. She's apologizing."

"Wow," I said. "Take it in—her tears, her apology."

Julie continued to cry.

"Can you tell your mother what her tears mean? What her apology means to you?" I asked.

Julie raised her gaze slowly. When we made eye contact, she smiled. A long pause followed. "Her apology means everything," she said.

"Can you close your eyes and tell her what you just said to me?" I asked. "Just imagine she's sitting right here." I pointed to an empty chair beside Julie.

Julie closed her eyes and turned to the empty chair. "Mom, thank you for this apology." Her breathing was deep, slow, and steady.

I waited a moment before speaking. "Is there more to say?"

"Not really," she said, and opened her eyes.

"We touched on something important today," I said, gazing into her eyes. "Know and honor your feelings as you continue to grapple with trusting your mother. What happened when you were a teenager was opened up here today. I trust you can sit with all that continues to come up, and your body will help you know what needs to happen next."

I asked Julie to take a few more breaths before she made eye contact with the larger group. After debriefing her and giving her the opportunity to hear how her work touched many of the workshop participants, I turned my attention to the teaching piece. I explained how we all carry unhealed pain, which can and will be ignited at any time. As therapists, we must help our patients learn to sit with their pain, and our own capacity to sit with pain can further help our patients. While we are wired to run from pain and sitting with it feels counterintuitive, being present with our pain and knowing how to manage it are the behaviors we need to model. This is an important resource for all of us, as therapists, patients, and parents. Our ability to self-regulate is what we pass on to our patients—and our children.

Mother Knows Best

It was 1981. I was with my six-year-old daughter, Rachel, shopping for a gift for my mother's sixty-third birthday. Rachel spotted a small velvet throw pillow trimmed in royal blue.

"Do you think Grandma would like that?"

Royal blue is my mother's favorite color, but it's the words stitched in pale blue wool that stand out: "Mirror, mirror, on the wall, I am my mother after all." I'd vowed to mother my own children differently from the way I'd been mothered, unaware that we are unconsciously wired by our early childhood experiences. It would take me a long time to understand that even with hard work on ourselves, we are all prisoners prone to repeat the past. I had no way of knowing I would inadvertently follow in my mother's footsteps, more than once.

Four years earlier, it had been a hot and humid August day on Long Island, and I was sitting on the beach with my mother and Rachel, who was two, when my old college friend Barbara arrived, escaping the heat wave suffocating Manhattan. Sheltered by a huge umbrella, Rachel was engrossed, digging in the sand. Barbara was recently divorced, and I hadn't seen her in almost a year. I was itching for a few moments of privacy to catch up and hear how life was unfolding for her. When Barbara suggested the two of us take a walk on the beach my mother agreed to watch Rachel.

"Just sneak away when she's busy," she whispered. "If you tell her you're leaving, she'll probably have a tantrum. If you just take off, she'll never even know you're gone."

Something inside me rumbled. I should have listened to my body, but instead of following my gut, I stood up quietly and snuck off with Barbara. I couldn't have been more than fifty feet away when I looked back to see how Rachel was doing. There she was, sitting on my mother's lap, screaming. Leaving Barbara at the water's edge, I turned and raced back to my daughter. As I neared, she spotted me and flew out of my mother's arms and into mine.

"Mommy," she wailed, as we sat on the scorching sand, "where were you? Why didn't you tell me you were going away?"

I hugged my screaming girl, dried her tears, and settled her down. Then I looked over at my mother. "I shouldn't have walked away without telling her where I was going." I added, "That's not the right thing to do, Ma."

"Don't worry," my mother said. "She'll get over it. You used to scream bloody murder when I left you."

It took me a minute to absorb what she had said. "I screamed bloody murder when you left me," I repeated. "So, if you knew she'd be so upset, why did you tell me to sneak away?"

My mother shrugged. "I knew you wanted to take a walk with Barbara, and I knew she'd get over it. She'll get over it, dear; we get over everything, dear. You certainly did. Don't worry so much. She'll be fine."

My mother had capped off her speech with her signature lines: "She'll get over it. We all get over everything. She'll be fine."

Sitting there, glaring at my mother and rocking my daughter, I bit my lip so as not to explode. What kind of horrible advice had I gotten from my mother, once again? But not only was I angry with her, I was livid at myself, critical and ashamed of my poor judgment. By the time I left Rachel on the beach that sticky August day, I was already familiar with my mother's cavalier child-rearing philosophy. Years of my own psychoanalysis had unearthed the childhood roots of my insecurities. I had even come to understand that my mother had never meant to be harmful. She'd done the best she could, and, as she described it, she was simply a product—or a victim—of her generation.

But my frustration ran deeper than my anger at my mother. In addition to ignoring what I'd learned from my own therapy, I was now a graduate student studying psychology, drenched in child-development theories, which across the board stressed the importance of parents' creating a secure attachment as a prerequisite for healthy growth. Nonetheless, I had ignored my instincts and listened to my mother. In essence, although I'd sworn never to be like her, I had blithely and blindly followed in her footsteps.

While my life work as a therapist certainly supports my belief that growth and change are always possible, two caveats should be noted. Without hard work on ourselves, we are doomed to repeat the past, and, even when we do our difficult inner work, the road to reconstructing oneself is bumpy, filled with unexpected potholes. It's taken me decades to understand the limitations of psychological insight and to respect the fact that insight can be hijacked so easily by our early programming. And my early programming—true for most of us—is not what I learned in my twenties as a psychotherapy patient or in my thirties as a graduate student, but rather what I learned as a small child who yearned for my mother's love and approval. Driven to please her, I absorbed and internalized her essence. Unconsciously, a part of me was still devoted to the voice in my head whispering, *"Mother knows best."*

Judy, Daughter of Peggy: Captain of the Cheerleaders, Always Smiling

I am Judy, daughter of Peggy, captain of the cheerleaders, always smiling.

When I was twelve, my grandma Sophie took me to the Broadway production of *The Diary of Anne Frank*. Sitting in the dark, I was mesmerized by the scared young girl, my age, writing in her journal. Just like I was, she was outspoken. Unlike me, she was trapped in a secret room, hiding from the Nazis. By the time the knock came on the annex door and the curtain fell, I was overcome with grief.

After we left the theater, we headed to the Long Island Railroad station. On the train home, my grandmother opened her huge, overflowing purse. First, she took out a special candy bar for us to share. Next, came a bottle of water. Finally, she handed me a wrapped package.

"A gift for you," she said, placing it in my hands.

"Grandma! You've already given me the best gift in the world—taking me to this show!" I handed the package back to her.

Gently but insistently, she handed the meticulously wrapped gift back to me. When I unwrapped it, I gasped. It was a small white leather diary with a lock and a tiny brass key.

The next day, I began my first journal.

———————

Like my heroine Anne, I also called that first diary Kitty. Kitty became my faithful listener, a space of my own in which to ponder and record my secrets—a place I could turn to when my heart was full, when my brain was exploding, when I felt misunderstood or alone.

Within a month, I was a conscientious journal writer. I understood that Anne and I were worlds apart; she'd lived in a terrifying universe where the threat of starvation, imprisonment, and death hovered over her, while I was ensconced in an upscale Long Island suburb where shopping for cashmere sweaters and cutting Hebrew school were my daily fare. Still, I felt deeply connected to Anne. I so admired her. Not only was she courageous, surviving in life-threatening circumstances, but she boldly scoffed at her mother.

"Did you know that Anne's mother didn't really understand her?" I asked my mother one day. I was sitting in the kitchen, and my mother was preparing a rainbow Jell-O dessert. "Anne had to hide her thoughts and feelings from everyone. She had to keep what really mattered secret."

"Secret? She kept secrets? What kind?" my mother asked. "Wasn't the whole family crammed into a small space? I would think everyone knew everyone else's business!"

"What does one thing have to do with another, Ma? You can't keep secrets even though you live in a small space?" I am sure she heard—and ignored—my sarcasm. *How could my mother be so simpleminded?* I wondered. "You do remember that she and her mother kept having run-ins?"

"Run-ins?"

"You saw the play, right, Ma?"

My mother nodded, but I could tell she was distracted by her Jell-O mold.

"Did you read the book, Ma?" By now, I was frustrated. Only days after we saw the play, my grandmother had brought me a copy of the book. I'd devoured it in a day, and when I finished it, I'd offered it to my mother to read.

"I have to admit," my mother said apologetically, "I started reading it, but I didn't get a chance to finish."

How, I wondered, was it possible for her to put down this amazing book that had so totally absorbed me?

It was as if she could read my mind. "I really was enjoying it, but I've been so busy. Commitments matter, Judy, and I promised to take a new dessert to the garden-club luncheon next week."

I looked over at her with what I can only imagine was yearning, but I could see her attention was still riveted on the packets of Jell-O lined up on the countertop, waiting to be transformed into her new dessert recipe.

She sighed. "I thought this rainbow Jell-O recipe would be simple, but each of these six boxes is an individual project," she said, as she swept her arm across the counter and pointed to the small square packages broadcasting their flavors: lime, raspberry, black cherry, strawberry, mint green, and lemon. "Each has to be prepared and layered in the mold separately. It's not simple, and it's *very* time-consuming," she added. "Each packet goes into a separate pot of boiling water, one at a time. Then, after each pot cools down to room temperature, it has to be poured into the mold, evenly. Then it has to be refrigerated until it gels—the next layer can't go into the mold until the one beneath it hardens. This is to prevent the colors from bleeding into one another. . .."

My mother continued talking, but I had disappeared. Obviously, there was no way I could compete with her rainbow Jell-O recipe. I had no way of knowing that the seeds of my identity were solidifying and a gap was developing. I was determined I'd never be like her—obsessed with stupid recipes. Thank goodness I had my Kitty.

"People don't like to hear your troubles."

I'd heard my mother utter these words repeatedly, and her message was clear: "Don't complain, and don't bother people—or me." I knew she would dismiss my worries if I tried to share them with her. Writing was one way I learned to take care of myself when I was scared, confused, or lonely. Over the next six decades, I became a persistent, compulsive writer, filling spiral notebooks and eventually more elegant, cloth-covered books with my inner musings, joys and sorrows, woes and sufferings.

My mother's personal stamp was her smile and her Pollyanna spirit. She was warm and fun-loving, and whatever went on, she was always able to see the upside. I'll never forget the one story she loved to tell about me; perhaps the way she told it said as much about her as it did about me.

When I was four, I fell in love with a pair of red boots. After I nagged my mother for weeks, one rainy day she caved and took me to the fanciest shoe store in our town. As soon as the salesman slipped my little feet into those red boots, I jumped off the bench and ran out of the store into the rain. Running up and down the street, I darted in and out of the raindrops, splashing in puddles until I was soaked, covered with mud and rain. The way my mother told this story made it clear what a kick she got out of her spunky, rambunctious child—even though, she'd always add that the spots on my clothing never came out. "They were a permanent reminder of my wild Judy," she'd say, with a smile.

To her dying day, she told the story of my red boots and spoke about her marvelous parents and her perfect childhood.

Her perpetual optimism irritated me until the end, but I have to admit, even now, there was something appealing about her easygoing nature.

Above my desk, I keep a picture that reminds me of her sunny disposition. In the photograph, my parents are on a motorcycle and my mother is snuggled into my father's chest, smiling, circa 1945. My handsome father, once captain of the football team, is now in the army. He nestles my beautiful, chic mother, once the captain of the cheerleaders, in his arms. My dad is dressed in a striking army uniform. He'd been stationed in Sioux City, South Dakota, and had been granted a two-day furlough. My mother had taken a three-day train trip to meet him for the weekend. Sitting on their bed as a child, I stared at this photograph, captivated by this image of romance and joyful exuberance. Someday, I hoped, I'd grow up, and if I were lucky, I'd be swept off my feet and get married to a handsome man with a motorcycle!

My mother was born in 1918, two years before women won the right to vote. Although I didn't think much about this until recently, this historical fact was part of a fabric that shaped the lives of her generation of women.

My mother was the only child of Lillian Baer and Henry Lipschutz. Being an only child was one of the few things I ever heard her grumble about—though she didn't really complain. Occasionally, she would admit that being an only child brought with it a certain kind of loneliness, but, true to form, she would underscore the benefits: As an only child, she was "spoiled rotten." According to her story, she was determined to spare me her fate; four years after I was born, she gave birth to my younger brother, John. Throughout her life, whenever it came time for a toast, she would inevitably stress how proud she was of the strong friendship her two children had, something that she had always yearned for. To this day, my brother remains one of my closest friends. To this day, I thank her for bestowing her wish upon us. To this day, I am reminded that wounds can be transformed into gifts.

My mother's optimism colored her world. When I asked her (which I did repeatedly) why her mother, my grandma Lillian, had only one child, the only answer I could ever get from her was a shrug. She didn't know, and it didn't seem to bother her that she didn't know. "I guess Grandma couldn't have more children," she would respond, with little emotion. Thinking back, I realize that infertility and miscarriage were taboo subjects—as was the topic of unwanted pregnancies. My mother was born not only before women had the vote, but also in an era when people didn't talk about "those things." Curiosity—if it existed—was something one kept to oneself. It was an era when people didn't ask each other personal questions, which could have been construed as prying, rather than expressing interest or concern.

My grandpa Henry, my mother's father, was a dress manufacturer. He grew up in Virginia, rumor has it his father fought for the South in the Civil War. He was twelve years older than Grandma Lillian, who grew up in Hoosick Falls, New York, a small town thirty miles north of Albany. Lillian's father owned the general store, and at twenty-one, in 1914, Lillian received a bachelor of arts from Syracuse University. Having a college degree was quite unusual for a woman in those days, but my grandmother's uniqueness was minimized in my home. Four years after graduation, she was married to Grandpa Henry and, within the year, gave birth to my mother.

Coming from the families they did, both of my parents were college bound. High school sweethearts, my father and mother had been accepted to Dartmouth and to Goucher College respectively. Then, in their senior year of high school, when they were both eighteen, fate intervened—my mother became pregnant. In lieu of college, they eloped on the East End of Long Island in the summer of 1936. Shortly afterward, they left for Salisbury, Maryland, where my father, tutored by his uncle Ben, learned the ropes of the family shirt-manufacturing business. My mother devoted herself to preparing for a baby and setting up their apartment.

Within two months, she miscarried.

For most of my adolescence, I romanticized their relationship—and idealized their elopement. When I was leaving for college, my father warned me to "be careful," a euphemism for using birth control and avoiding pregnancy. Only then did I learn the truth about the pregnancy that changed the course of their lives.

I was born in 1942, six years after my parents married. When I was ten months old, my father went into the army and my grandparents moved into my parents' home in Hewlett, on Long Island. As the first grandchild, described always as a precocious, adorable, and energetic little girl, I followed in my mother's footsteps and was "spoiled rotten" by my mother and my grandparents. All that was about to change, however. In 1946, my father returned home from the army, my grandparents moved to their own apartment and shortly thereafter, my brother was born. My charmed life as a little princess at the center of the universe came to an end.

In 1972, when my mother was fifty-four and I was thirty, my strong, virile father died unexpectedly after a short bout with bladder cancer. A year later, my mother remarried, only to lose her second husband, Lenny, to a massive heart attack one year after that. By the time she was sixty-one, she would bury Herbert, her partner of five years. After Herbert's death, when asked if she was looking for another man, she would respond with a pithy, upbeat line that always got a laugh: "Three husbands is enough, and anyway, why bother? At my age, what men want is nurses with purses."

About my mother's defining Pollyanna optimism: Certainly, it provided her with a core of resilience that helped her face disappointment, loss, death, and her own eventual battle with Parkinson's disease. She reminded me of one of my favorite heroines, Scarlett O'Hara, who had lost the man she loved and her home by the end of *Gone With the Wind*, but stood at the top of the staircase and was able to say, "Tomorrow is another day."

But when I was growing up, her "sunny nature," as she called it, was problematic for me. We were out of sync, and I knew it. As a child, I found refuge in books, where I was eagerly absorbed into and fascinated by a wider, darker universe. As an adolescent, I was angry, disgusted by my mother's inability to acknowledge anything less than happiness. I spent decades—to no avail—wanting her to acknowledge the more difficult and challenging sides of life, hers and mine, but, regardless of how I approached her, getting her to do so was impossible. After all, this was a woman for whom nothing about her parents ever rubbed her the wrong way. They were flawless.

"You're kidding me, Ma!" I would say when I got older.

"You don't want to believe me, but we didn't ever fight."

"Not even when you were a teenager?"

"About what?"

"Didn't you ever break their rules?"

"Rules? Like what?"

"Coming home late?"

She would shake her head and remain resolute. Whatever happened, they worked it out.

This was the conversation we had over and over, with no resolution.

There was some way in which my mother seemed inauthentic that felt unbearable to me. When she insisted on a superficial happiness that lacked complexity, I felt alone in my suffering. Not until I began studying psychology and was introduced to the concept of interiority was I able to identify what was missing. Over time, I would come to accept that she would always choose the rainbow Jell-O mold over *The Diary of Anne Frank*.

Not even my second husband, Larry, who referred to himself as the Prince of Darkness, could draw her out of her uncanny ability to see the bright side of almost everything. Larry and I found each other when I was long divorced and over fifty; what drew me to him was his capacity to appreciate life's darkness and my pain. Throughout our marriage, he reminded me that my genuine tears were what initially touched him about me.

"'Perfect parents' sounds impossible, Peg. Almost suspicious," Larry told her one night over dinner.

"Well, it's the truth—they *were* perfect!" was my mother's automatic comeback. Not even Larry's formidable persistence could get through the vision she was wedded to.

Through many painful losses in our lives, I never saw my mother shed a tear. I don't know that she wasn't sad—I imagine she was—but she was simply not given to showing her emotions. In contrast with me, a crier, she was a mismatch. Whenever I asked her if anything—including the deaths of three husbands—bothered her, she would look at me blankly and assure me that each death had been a devastating loss but that she was not interested in looking backward.

"What's the point in complaining or going over the past?" was her usual response. "People don't like to hear your troubles" was another favorite. I frequently think about these crumbs of "wisdom" my mother offered. I wanted so much for her to hear my distress, to acknowledge my pain. I guess it makes perfect sense that listening to the troubles of others would become my life's work. Often we thrive when we can give others exactly what we yearn for most.

In the mother-daughter workshop, I was floored by the memory of my mother's betrayal and insensitivity at the time of my tonsillectomy, and all the pain from that childhood experience came flooding back. But that trauma, I came to understand, had so much power for me as an adult because it was emblematic of a larger blight in my relationship with my mother.

PART TWO:

The Secret

Close your eyes and think about a secret that was kept from you. Breathe deeply. Who kept the secret from you? How did you feel when the secret was revealed? If nothing comes to mind, perhaps a secret you hold has emerged. Think about a secret you keep or maybe have kept. Focus on the feelings that come up. Where does your body feel that secret? What is the sensation it causes in your muscles? What feelings and associations arise?

Kindred Spirits

It is the day after the Healing the Mother-Daughter Relationship workshop. After a mad dash through the busy Columbus, Ohio, airport, I am relieved to be settled into my window seat on United flight 405, headed for JFK. Snuggling into my warm down coat, I gaze out the window into the blackness. I cannot stop thinking about my conversation this morning with Julie. After not speaking to her mother for ten months, she picked up the phone and called her, and now they're planning a visit. I feared doing personal work in front of the group might destabilize her, but the opposite seems to be true; it motivated her to take action. Even without my knowing the details of how their communication broke down, Julie feels like a kindred spirit. Her sense of betrayal and the damage that can flow in the wake of family secrets resonate with me.

Whiteout

Forehead smack up against the icy plane window, I'm lost in an old memory, an image of whirling snowflakes drifting down onto the sidewalk. I feel them melting against my cheeks. I see my mother and me waiting for the light to change so we can cross the street. That moment, as we stood on the street corner, is blown up in my mind. The red traffic light shimmered in the wetness while we waited for it to turn to green. I was wearing the lamb-trimmed brown shearling coat my parents had given me for my thirtieth birthday, the last birthday we shared before my father was diagnosed with the terminal cancer that took him, the funeral just three weeks ago today. An early death at fifty-four. That was the last birthday I celebrated before my family fairy tale exploded.

"You don't have to take such good care of me, Judy. I have someone."

"You have someone?"

"I'm not alone."

"What do you mean, Ma?"

"I have a boyfriend." Her mouth was still open; her words rang in my ears.

That image is frozen. A huge smile was spread across her face, and her skin was radiant. Her red lipstick glistened.

"I have someone, I have someone. I have a man . . . I guess I should call him my boyfriend."

I saw her mouth move. I heard her speak. She was in the foreground; I was in the shadows.

I cannot remember how I felt or what I said as I heard the details. Did I take in that all the time we were waiting for my father to die, she had her Mr. Affair hovering in the wings, and now that the coast was clear, now that my father had been gone for three weeks, my mother was free?

I must have felt a lot. I can't remember, though. Was there an agonizing cry stuck in my throat? Did I calmly ask questions, walk side by side with her to my building? How did we get on the elevator and end up in the living room of my seventh-floor apartment?

Here is what I do remember. Before she departed, Andrea, the babysitter told me that my five-month-old son, Zach, had just gone down for a nap. The door banged shut, and my mother and I were alone. Bustling, my mother put her things down and settled onto my nubby tweed living-room couch. Not wanting to look at her, I turned away, my eyes drawn to a photograph of my parents when they were young. It was the same photograph that sat on my mother's dresser when I grew up; my father was sitting on the motorcycle, smiling, holding my mother, who was also smiling. My eyes locked with my father's.

"Who is he, Ma? What's his name?" *Is this really my voice?*

"I can't tell you. Yet."

"Yet. Why?"

"Because he's still married. I gave him my word I wouldn't tell anyone who he is until he leaves his wife."

I heard my own breath, racing in and out in the silence.

My mother has a boyfriend. A man who is going to leave his wife for her, now that she is free.

"Free" was the word she used. This was not a word I would have thought to use to describe my mom. But I had to face it—she was a widow, and while I thought she was in mourning, she thought of herself as free.

I was still facing away from her, looking at my father's face. "When did you meet him?"

She giggled.

This was the first time since my father had been gone that I had heard her laugh in this girlish way—the way I imagined she laughed on the motorcycle.

"A long, long time ago," she said slowly.

"What's a long time?" I asked. My face was hot. I couldn't catch my breath.

"I've known him my whole life. Or it seems that way."

"Your whole entire life?"

"Not really my whole life, dear—that's just a figure of speech. But it seems we've been together forever. He's been good *to* me and very good *for* me. Very good, dear."

"Good for you," I growled, but she ignored the sarcasm in my voice. "So, how long have you been having this affair?"

"Eight years."

Eight years! I must have gasped. I counted backward. "You knew him when I got married?"

What came next was another level of insensitivity on her part, another level of pain for me. "Yes, I knew him when you and Arnie got married. In fact, he was at your wedding."

I moved away from her. I was woozy and light-headed. I turned toward the window; the snow had gathered inches high along the ledge.

"Do you love him?" I asked.

"I do." Her words slid out. Quickly. Not even a pause. Not even a glance at me.

I was numb, speechless. I couldn't allow myself to think my thoughts—my mother was shtupping Mr. Affair while the chemo was destroying my father's bones?

My thoughts cascaded as I saw her not so blithely shopping

for stockings for shiva—was she slipping out to a motel when I thought she was at the hairdresser? Was she eager to stop role-playing the devoted, loving wife? I said none of that. Instead I asked softly, "What do you want from me?"

She shrugged. "I thought you'd want to know that I'm not alone. You don't have to worry about me so."

That wasn't the answer I wanted. Why didn't she ask me about me—how was I doing with this new information? Wasn't she concerned about the impact of her affair on me? Did she suspect I was upset? Everything I believed about my parents had dissolved into the slushy snow.

"I'm lucky," she said.

My hands were cold, and I rubbed them together, trying to warm them. *Ask me how I am, Ma,* I wished, but she didn't ask.

"Who is he?" I could not help but ask again. Later, I would replay this scene, hundreds of times, and I would hear her tell me, "You don't have to worry about me. I have someone." I would see her red lips move. I would realize that I was irrelevant. The focus was on her: her happiness, her joy, her affair.

"I'm sorry, Judy, but I can't tell you. I promised him I wouldn't," she repeated.

"Did Daddy know about him?" I asked. Too much information poured out again. My father didn't know about *them,* but he knew *him.* She and my dad had met Mr. Affair when my brother was born, twenty-six years earlier. There were no single rooms available in the hospital the night she gave birth, so she wound up in a double room. Imagine that! Mr. Affair's wife was her roommate. What a stroke of luck!

"He has a son, too, one day younger than your brother. He's really wonderful, dear. You'll see when you meet him."

She must be kidding. She thinks I'm going to meet him? Then it dawned on me: *I've already met him. I might even know him well!*

"I must be going," she said. "Don't tell Arnie our little secret."

Of course I'm going to tell my husband. Who do you think I am—a lying bitch like you? That's what I felt like saying. Instead, I walked her to the door.

"Thank you for everything. You're a dear, a dear daughter," she said, giving me her perfunctory peck on the cheek. "And let's not tell John yet, either."

I turned off the light in my living room, sat down, and stared out at the falling snow. The sky was a whiteout, Zach was still sleeping, and my mother's secret burrowed in, drilling a hole in my heart.

Outside my window, the snow was coming down steadily, creating a magical wonderland, but inside, my mother's words deafened me, pounding and ringing: "*I have someone, I have someone. You don't have to take such good care of me; I have someone.*"

In only a matter of minutes, I had left the life I knew. My kingdom had been overthrown. My mind was awhirl.

I had thought it was my responsibility to take care of my mother. Why hadn't I told her what was on my mind?

Of course I have to take care of you, Ma! You're my responsibility now. Isn't that what you did for your mother when your father passed? Family takes care of one another, right, Ma? I remember Grandma Lillian moving in with us for a few months when Grandpa Henry died. You took care of your mother, and then, five years ago, you took care of me when Michael died. You didn't really know him well, but he was mine, my brand-new fiancé, and I was heartbroken. If not for you, I would have collapsed at the cemetery that freezing day in January. You stood by me and held me up at his funeral, where I was persona non grata. You were there when I felt like I couldn't go on.

"You're going to go on, Judy," you told me, *and you sounded so sturdy, so sure of yourself. I hated you for saying I would love again, but you were right. Less than two years later, I married Arnie.*

———————

When Arnie came home late that night, I was curled up in bed, lights off, feigning sleep. Not expecting to feel much comfort or relief from talking to my husband, I said nothing. These weeks since my father's death had been hard for us; I had felt disconnected from him. He had been wrapped up helping my mother straighten out her finances, but emotionally absent to me. Besides, I could not bear to repeat my mother's words.

I remember the sleepless night that followed. I lay awake, reviewing and replaying and reconstructing the past eight years of my life, searching for a crevice hiding Mr. Affair. The identity of my mother's lover obsessed me. Who could he be?

I remember sitting with Zach in the oak rocker, just rocking. My mother and I had bought and restored what we hoped was a genuine antique at the end of my pregnancy, when it was uncomfortable to stand or sit or sleep. Now, as I held my Zach close, the rocking soothed both of us. We watched the moon.

The next morning, as soon as Arnie left the house, I pulled out my fancy, gold-trimmed, white leather wedding album. Back in third grade, I'd been president of the Nancy Drew Club of Woodmere, Long Island, I reminded myself. I knew how to collect and analyze clues. The white leather book seemed like a reasonable place to begin my search, so there I sat on my living room floor, inspecting each picture for clues. How had I missed what should have been evident? What was right before my eyes? I scrutinized every male in every photo, searching for someone with a son the age of my brother, John. A wild goose chase. No leads.

The day she told me remains a blur. I remember walking around, dazed, torn apart. One part of me wanted to know every detail about my mother's romance. Another part of me longed to deny it. My father was dead, and my mother was dancing on his grave. I knew their marriage had been complicated—my father had been critical—sometimes even demeaning—but I hadn't realized the extent to which their marriage had been compromised. Was everything I'd grown up with a lie? Had my mother had other affairs? And what about my father, who was always away on business trips?

I can't say why I feigned sleep the night of my mother's big reveal, or how I finally decided—a day or two later—to gather my courage to tell my husband that my mother had a boyfriend. Arnie and I were sitting in the living room. He was engrossed, reading the newspaper, and I was aware that I couldn't concentrate on my book club selection, Margaret Mead's *Blackberry Winter*. I thought I would collapse if I didn't talk about it.

"Can you put down your newspaper?" I asked, with a deliberate softness, fearful of his reaction. Arnie hated being interrupted. So often, I had been unbalanced by his disdainful attitude toward me, and now I couldn't imagine what he would think about my mother. Perhaps I couldn't bear to see what I expected on his face. My heart pounded as I waited for his response.

No reaction. I started over. "Arnie, I want to tell you something. It's important. Your newspaper—please put it down," I repeated, more loudly.

He looked at me over the lowered Business section of the *New York Times* and said nothing. I saw only a tight scowl beneath flashing brown eyes and bushy eyebrows.

"What is it, Judith?" Whenever he called me Judith, I knew something was bothering him and he was taking it out on me. His voice was taut. His parents' divorce was, I knew, still raw. One year after our wedding, George, Arnie's father, had run off with his young secretary, Terry. It's an old story, but it was new for Arnie. I hated to burden him with my anguish; disregarding my needs was an old story for me.

My throat had closed down. I could hardly get the words out.

"I guess your parents weren't so happy, either," he said after I told him, and turned back to his newspaper. His words seared me, but I said nothing. I was starving and our marriage table was bare, but I hated begging for crumbs.

What I needed was a reassuring hug and his empathy. I wanted permission to cry. I wanted him to rock me like I rocked my Zach when he cried. But that's not what I got. I made excuses for him, rather than asking for what I wanted. I told myself that he was worn out, too, from my father's long illness and his death and from lack of sleep with Zach's crying. Worn out from working in an intense office with a demanding boss. Worn out because he was caught up in his parents' raging divorce battles that had dragged on and on these past three years.

If this were to happen today, I hope I would be different. I hope I would speak in my calmest, most mindful voice and say, "Dear, this isn't just about my parents. It's about me. It's about the life I thought I lived, the family I thought I grew up in, the mother I thought I knew." But back then, when I was less conscious than I am today, I didn't have the wherewithal to insist Arnie put down his fucking newspaper. Only later would I realize that we missed an opportunity to bond; dealing with our parents' unfaithfulness could have opened a conversation about what we both needed in our marriage. But that conversation didn't happen.

I fell into a routine. Zach went to sleep easily at 7:00 p.m. Somewhere between 1:00 and 3:00 a.m., his cries awakened me. I slipped out of my bed and picked him up. I looked at the moon and hummed. The top of his head was so soft; I nuzzled my nose into his thin blond hair. Eventually, after rocking my boy back to sleep, I poured myself a thimbleful of Dewar's, and then another, while my mind furiously replayed a conversation with my mother.

She and I were sitting in the kitchen in my apartment, and I had just finished feeding Zach his nighttime cereal. Now, as on every night of my life those days, his face and the highchair tray were smeared with the chunks of banana that hadn't made it into his mouth. The floor was littered, too, and I was feeding him and cleaning up while my mother and I sipped our chardonnay.

"It was a harmless affair, dear."

"An affair is harmless, Ma? Explain that to me!"

"I've told you already—I would never have left your father. I would never have broken up our family. What's most important to me is family—you know that."

"So why did you have an affair?"

"Judy, I don't like you putting me on the spot. I was sick of being criticized. Your dad was a difficult man. I loved him, even though he could be impossible, and you know that."

I did know that. He was critical, not only of her but of me.

"Did you and Dad ever try therapy?"

My mother scrunched up her face. "Therapy? Do you think your father would ever have gone to therapy? Don't you remember what he said when you wanted to go to therapy? Judy, you know how opinionated he was about everything— and he thought therapy was for the birds. I disagreed, but it was never easy for me to get him to see things my way. You know how hard I had to work on him before he agreed to pay for your therapy, right?"

I did remember and knew my mother was correct. She had a point, and she had gone to bat for me.

"Your father was a big boss, Judy—and . . ."

Even though I'd stopped listening, her words echoed, leaving me confused and sad. *Is infidelity the solution to marital boredom, Ma? Did you think of yourself as an adulteress?* I was surprised to hear those words in my head. I felt a tightening in my solar plexus, and I gasped for air. It was the first time the words "infidelity" and "adulteress" had surfaced—much stronger than the word "affair." Perhaps it was my own breath that opened up my mind. Suddenly, I remembered a box containing extra wedding photographs that was stored in my closet in the house where I grew up. Could my mother's lover be sitting in the pile?

Home Again

It was sunny and mild that Tuesday morning when I went out to my mother's house. Arnie was in Philadelphia on business for the day, and my mother was visiting her sister-in-law, my father's younger sister, Cecile, in West Palm Beach. As soon as Andrea, the babysitter, arrived, I kissed Zach goodbye and went to Pennn Station to catch the Long Island Railroad to the house I'd grown up in. I still had the key.

It wasn't until I was sitting in the Penn Station waiting room that my anxiety hit me. The radiators were sizzling, but I was freezing. My mouth was dry, and my head was throbbing when it dawned on me that I hadn't been back to the house since we had sat shiva for my father. Shiva had ended just a month earlier, and Zach had had one ear infection after another, which had kept me in the city. Just imagining being alone in the house without a soul there plunged me into darkness as I revisited my father's last days—the sound of his gasping for breath when the oxygen tank by his bed became useless. From my father's diagnosis until his death, Arnie had been loving and supportive. But lately, things had been miserable. We'd been fighting for weeks, and after our blowup the night before, I hadn't even told him I was going to Long Island today. I hadn't told my mother, either. I felt creepy sneaking around behind her back, but every time that phrase, "sneaking around behind her back," popped into my mind, I became infuriated. Why should I be feeling creepy when she'd been sneaking around behind my father's back for eight years?

"It's two houses before the cul-de-sac on the end," I told the cab driver, as we wound our way down Lefferts Road in Woodmere.

Slipping into the house, I quickly climbed the stairs. When I opened the door to the room that had been mine, the first thing I spotted was my Nancy Drew collection, those beautiful books bound in blue leather, their titles in orange. There they sat, neatly lined up on the bottom of my bookshelf. *I could sit here all day and reread those books and no one would know,* I thought, as I lay down on my old bed, staring at the curtains of my girlhood. This was the room where I'd dreamed I'd have strawberry-blond hair, a blue convertible, and a credit card, just like Ms. Nancy, my idol.

Closing my eyes, I was barraged by thoughts, images, and questions floating in and out about the life my parents had led—or the life I thought they'd led. Had my father known? How could he not have? But maybe he hadn't. Or maybe he had and chose not to acknowledge his marriage's shadowy truth, especially during his illness, when he needed my mother's devotion, even if it had to be on her terms.

I longed for the comforting sound of my dad's "rise and shine" whistle. How many weekend mornings had I been annoyed to be woken up too early? But now, how I wished I could once more be greeted with his melodic announcement that the sun had already been up for hours. What was the truth of my parents' marriage? And why was I procrastinating, lying on my bed, caught in a time warp, when the photograph boxes in the closet were beckoning to me?

Could it have been only a month ago that I'd been living in a fantasy about my family? Could it have been only two months ago that I'd had no idea how soon my father would die?

Bad News

Only three months earlier, my mother and I had been sitting at my dad's hospital bedside when we heard a knock on the door and Dr. Vacco walked in. My dad was dozing and the doctor motioned for my mother and me to step into the hall.

"I'm afraid . . ." His voice trailed off, his eyes lost in a downward gaze. He cleared his throat, looked my mother straight in the eye, and began again. "We got back the latest blood tests, and the results . . . the results indicate . . . there's really no point in continuing the chemo. I'm sad to share this bad news." Dr. Vacco's voice was soft, kind, and steady.

It took me a few minutes to process this wrenching news. My father was not getting better. No more tennis. No more ski trips. No more sailing with him in Long Island's shallow creeks and watching him happily wash down the boat at the end of the day. When we were kids, he took us sailing almost every weekend. Rough, stormy weather excited him; the windier the day, the better for him. Storms that terrified me, he would sail right into. He would pull in the mainsail, tighten the jib, and heel, letting the wind grab and tug at the mainsail as he grabbed and tugged back. He loved to lean back over the water with the sail spread out tight and full in front of him, ease out the main sheet, and grin as the boat heeled and the water flapped at the deck and spilled over the sides.

And there was more. He had a soft and sensitive side. He adored the opera. Now, there would be no more sitting together, listening to his favorites, Puccini and Verdi, and following the librettos. Saturday afternoons in the winter, when sailing was out, he'd sit in the living room, listening to *Tosca*, *La Bohème*, and *Madame Butterfly* on the hi-fi.

"Judy, come here!" he'd bellow. "Come sit with me; hear how beautiful this is!" Often he'd have tears in his eyes. Together we'd sit side by side, following the libretto, listening to the glorious arias together, as he passed on his passion to me. And now it was over.

From the onset, I had known where my father's bladder cancer would end. I'd been at my cousin Winnie's, celebrating my thirtieth birthday, when my mother had called. "It didn't go well today," she whispered, and I knew that the "it" referred to my father's monthly checkup. My mother had been going with him to these appointments; his bladder cancer surgery had been only four months earlier.

When Dad was getting dressed after the examination, the oncologist had called my mother into his office. "It's spread. The cancer is everywhere, Judy," were my mother's exact words. My father wasn't going to recover. The doctor thought it best not to share this bad news with him, at least not right then. It didn't matter that in May, the surgeon had told us otherwise. "You're damn lucky—I think we got it early enough, got it all out," he'd said. We had even heard the magic words "clean margins." But now, only months later, the cancer had spread—to his lungs and his brain.

It had begun to snow by the time we left the hospital that night. We were on the Long Island Expressway, stuck in bumper-to-bumper traffic, when my mother announced she wasn't feeling much like going home right away.

"Honey, let's stop at Shurries," she suggested, referring to her favorite boutique. "They sent out a flyer. If I remember correctly, good, high-quality stockings are on sale this week. And God knows, with a shiva coming—you never know when—stockings are a good thing to have on hand. And you can't beat their prices: six pairs for ten dollars. I think they're Hanes first quality, but who knows? You never know when you're getting seconds."

I was speechless. *Dad isn't going to beat his cancer, and she's trying to get a bargain on the price of stockings to wear to his funeral and shiva—and worrying about whether they're firsts or seconds? How disgusting!* "Ma, are you kidding me? You're talking about bargains?"

"It will only take a minute, Judy. I'll be in and out." She pulled off the road into Shurrie's parking lot and opened the car door. Why I followed her into the store, I cannot say. Within moments, she had grabbed several packages of stockings for both of us and we were standing at the cash register, ready to pay for them.

"I'm not crazy about those gloves you've been wearing, honey," she said, referring to the handmade Peruvian mittens I'd picked up on my backpacking trip before I married Arnie. "They really don't go with your new coat. What about these?" She pointed to a pair of soft brown leather gloves she'd picked up. "Here," she said, plucking them off the counter and handing them to me. "Try them on; see if they fit. It's my treat!"

Remembering my mission, the photograph boxes, I slipped off the bed and opened the closet door. Treasured clothing from every era of my life was jammed in there: fancy taffeta skirts I'd worn to proms, two wool swing coats, T-shirts and tennis dresses and running pants. I spotted my old red ski parka and ski gloves, the ones I used to wear when my dad and I skied the black diamond trails. I suddenly felt like retching, over-whelmed by my yearning for the past, for my father, for the life I thought I'd led, the family I thought I'd had.

I was on my knees, peering into the back of my childhood closet, looking for boxes of photos from my wedding so I could unearth the mystery of my mother's longtime lover. Just as I'd imagined, the two shoeboxes were still tucked away, no tops, filled with a jumble of photographs. Carefully, I pulled out the fraying cardboard boxes and dumped the pictures onto the worn carpet in this room that had once been mine, back when I admired Nancy Drew more than anyone in the world.

Poring through the extra photos that hadn't made it into the album was more overwhelming than I'd anticipated. I was looking at a huge moment: my wedding day. It had been only three years earlier, yet everything I thought I knew felt unre-al—a corroded fantasy. I was surrounded by pictures, people dancing and talking and toasting. I could hear the champagne glasses clinking. I could see the smiling, laughing faces of friends and family: Cousin Harry, Uncle Jeffrey—and there was Adina, from my kindergarten class! I saw and heard the camera click-ing away. Dozens of photos of happy loved ones—what a day! I had to ignore how I was feeling now to go on with what I needed to do. As I pulled the pictures out of the boxes, I placed them carefully on the beige carpet, and a voice in my head egged me on to evaluate each image before me. After a careful look, I stacked the pictures into two piles, "no" and "maybe," while I simultaneously reconstructed family trees, searching for the father in the family that had a boy my brother John's age.

Combing through the pictures, I felt dizzy, remembering the endless circles of connections: Arnie's and my old friends, neighborhood friends, members of the synagogue and boat club, old friends of my parents, and relatives I had rarely seen before or since the wedding. I tried not to stray and to stay with the men: sons and fathers and uncles and . . .

All of a sudden, I saw him.

The picture might have looked innocent enough to anyone else, but not to me, once I saw the telltale image. In this picture, my mother was held snugly by a tall, balding man, a family friend who, I was now sure, was Mr. Affair. The two of them smiled straight into the camera.

The image glared at me. As my mom leaned in to this man, she was tilting her head and wearing the same coy smile she had in the motorcycle picture with my dad.

There he was, Mr. Affair. The tall, balding man, Lenny Nash, was my parents' insurance broker. Len's wife, Elaine, was the nurse in the office of my pediatrician, Dr. Steinman. Elaine, who had always held my hand and calmed me down when I got shots. Elaine, who had been present when Dr. Steinman mentioned the tonsillectomy to my mother. Elaine, whose son, Rob, played the drums in the band with my brother. Elaine, who carpooled my brother to band and baseball when my mother wasn't around. And now, the phrase "wasn't around" had new meaning.

I sat on the floor, gazing at this picture, for a long, long time. There was no one to speak to, and what would I have said, anyway? Eventually I jammed all the pictures back in the boxes, except this one, which I placed carefully in the inside zippered pouch of my tan nylon pocketbook.

Before I left, I climbed back into the closet, restacked all the photo boxes neatly, shut the closet door, and called for a taxi. *My father is dead, and none of this matters*, I told myself, as I put that photo in my purse. Except that my mother was still very much alive, and so was her secret. Alive in my heart.

I stood downstairs by the front door, waiting for the taxi to take me back to the Long Island Railroad station. I was sweating, even though the house was chilly. Peering out the window, awaiting the cab's headlights, I suddenly remembered how cold my hands were on the train ride out here. Had I been in an unheated car or just anxious? I walked over to the antique oak cabinet and opened the bottom drawer, which had forever been a home to assorted winter gloves and hats, scarves and earmuffs. I was immediately drawn to a worn, brown leather glove that belonged to my dad. A quick scrounge in the pile, and voilà! I came across its mate, which I brought to my lips. Its mate. The phrase saddened me. I slipped my hands into my father's gloves. In the worn pile lining, my fingers soaked him up. I breathed in the scent of his aftershave. The softness of his gloves reminded me of other gloves: the fur-lined pair I wore to his funeral; the gloves I was wearing when my mother revealed that she had been cheating on him for years and wasn't a bit sorry about it. Slipping the gloves into my coat pocket, I saw the taxi's headlights and slammed the front door behind me as I headed home to my husband and baby boy.

Marriage Gets Boring

I couldn't stop thinking about the picture of my mother at my wedding, arm in arm with her lover, Lenny Nash. When I emptied the dishwasher, when I fed Zach, as I walked to the subway to take the train to my graduate school classes at City College uptown, as I sat in the library trying to study, my mind kept wandering back to the photograph in the zippered pouch of my purse. I couldn't resist pulling it out and looking at it dozens of times. Every time I stared at that smile on my mom's face and noticed the way she nestled into Lenny's arm around her shoulder, I knew I was right. It was him.

Finally, I picked up my phone.

"Okay, Ma, it's Lenny Nash, right?"

"Judy, you've always been like a dog with a bone. I should have known it wouldn't take you long to figure this out." She could have denied it, insisted that she couldn't reveal his identity. She didn't ask how I'd figured it out. She didn't ask how I felt. She didn't seem to be the least bit ruffled about violating her vow of secrecy to Mr. Affair. In fact, she seemed relieved that I'd figured it and now could be her confidant. Perhaps she was even thankful to be able to discuss him openly with me.

"So, Ma, why did you get involved with Lenny?"

"Involved? I told you, I met him at St. Joseph's Hospital, when his wife and I gave birth, to your brother and to his son. Elaine was my roommate. Our boys were born within twelve hours of each other."

My heart was pounding. "That's not what I asked, Ma. I know that's how you met—you've told me this story already. I'm asking you something different. Why exactly did you get involved? Why, Ma? Why did you get involved—I mean, have an affair?" By now, my voice had risen. Beads of sweat were gathering everywhere—on my forehead, under my arms.

She said nothing.

"How did your affair begin?" It had taken me days to ask the questions that had been flooding my mind since I'd found that picture of her and Mr. Affair. Only now did I realize how frustrated I was. My mother was allergic to thinking through my questions. She was oblivious to her impact on me.

"There was nothing so much wrong with your father, Judy. Yes, he was difficult, not easy to live with, but it wasn't just that. It's just that marriage gets boring." She sighed. "And we were married so young." She sounded blasé.

"*So young?* What does that have to do with having an affair with Lenny?"

"You wouldn't understand, dear. You've been married for only three years. And you married Arnie when you were almost twenty-six. You had other boyfriends—boyfriends galore! When you were in college, I was married. When you went to school in France in your junior year, I was in Maryland with your father. I got married at eighteen. Eighteen! By the time I got involved with Len, I had been married for more than twenty-five years, honey! Married to your father, a pretty dominating, difficult man. I'm not making an excuse, but it gets boring, marriage does."

Her words scared me. I had been married for only three years, and I, too, found my husband dominating and difficult, far more controlling than he appeared when we first met. I reassured myself that while Arnie might be difficult, he was definitely not "boring." We had a new baby, and I was immersed in diapers and sleep schedules and endless rocking and soothing, and I had just started a playgroup with a neighbor. New motherhood had been mostly wondrous and mesmerizing, and, yes, sometimes boring, too, but our marriage? Challenging and more difficult than I'd imagined, but not boring.

"Did you consider talking to Daddy about how dogmatic he was? About how tedious it gets having the same arguments and discussions, with no movement?" I asked.

By the tone of my mother's voice, I knew she had put up a wall. She ignored my question, my intent to investigate; she answered calmly, patronizingly with a bit of disinterest. She seemed so self-assured. As my questions flew out of my mouth, I thought about the repetitive glitches I got into with Arnie, how frustrating our "talks" often were, how they often broke down into angry barbs and chilly withdrawals that hurt and stung and lasted too long. I took refuge in talking to my girlfriends and, thankfully, my analyst, Dr. Saxe. I wondered if my mother had ever confided her marital troubles to a friend, or if she and her friends skimmed life's darkness and spoke exclusively of recipes and clothes shopping.

"You didn't answer me, Ma. Did you consider talking to Daddy about what bothered you?"

My mother sighed. "Your father, dear—he wasn't the easiest person to communicate with. He wasn't good with expressing or talking about feelings. He wasn't a monster, but he wasn't from the listeners."

Not a monster? Why was she so defensive?

"Of course, he wasn't a monster, Ma! What does a monster have to do with anything?"

"You do know how difficult he was. And how different we were!" The word "difficult" jarred me, as did "different."

I wondered how I'd married Arnie—what had attracted me to him, given that our differences were now so glaring. I had stumbled into a minefield. I had always wanted to be different from my mother, to be independent and intellectually adventurous in ways that she wasn't, but it turned out that, like her, I had inadvertently—perhaps unconsciously—married a high-maintenance, controlling man who felt threatened by my ideas and needs.

"Different about what?" I asked warily.

"About everything! And mostly his ideas won out, right? Come on, Judy, you know how dominating he was—how he could argue and always win! You saw how bossy he was about everything. Everything!"

Her words hit home; unfortunately, I was fast becoming experienced with dealing with Arnie's bossiness. Just the night before, we'd been caught in a long, drawn-out argument about something so trivial I could barely remember what had gotten us started. I knew my father could be tyrannically stubborn. But I also thought of him as smart, opinionated, and sensitive, unlike my mother, who seemed to be a passive, silent follower with few thoughts of her own. Although now, of course, I knew that was just a pretense. She'd actually been very active, at least behind Dad's back.

"Okay, Ma, dealing with a big boss is a pain in the neck—I know that. Arnie is a big boss, too—at least, he tries to be. Did you think of therapy?"

Arnie had been in therapy when I met him, which was one of the things that had attracted me to him. I'd hoped he would be the introspective partner I dreamed of, but over time I had come to face what turned out to be more of the reality—therapy may have offered him a place to vent, not necessarily to reflect and change himself. So often, people go into therapy to change others, instead of working on themselves. While he kept to himself what happened in his sessions, for the most part what I witnessed was that, despite therapy, he became bossier and more controlling than ever. Often I thought I'd like to have a session with him and his therapist, but whenever I suggested it, Arnie stonewalled me.

My mother had already made it clear that according to my father, therapy wasn't what "people" did back then—but I knew that wasn't the truth. My uncle Victor was a renowned psychoanalyst, and my cousins Barbara and Winnie had already been in therapy. Concepts like the superego and the Freudian slip had already entered mainstream conversation, even on Long Island. But according to my mother, my dad wouldn't have considered going to a therapist. His philosophy, which I'd heard hundreds of times, was "There's nothing that a little fresh air doesn't cure!" According to him, a good game of tennis or a walk on the beach could fix any kind of distress.

"I never would have left your father for Lenny. Even though your father was bossy and difficult, I wouldn't have left him, not for Lenny or for anyone. I would never have broken up our family. Anyway, dear, he's gone, and the affair was harmless. I'm with Lenny, and there's no point in discussing the past, in discussing things that can't be changed."

"Harmless?" I echoed. I knew my voice was sarcastic. To me, an affair wasn't harmless. To me, an affair meant you'd decided it was fine to deceive your husband and to let your relationship with him drift, maybe disintegrate. But my mother was impenetrable.

"Harmless because I loved your father, and had he lived, we'd still be together, happily married." She reminded me that, despite his bossiness and his patriarchal values, my dad had been a good husband, an excellent provider, and a loving father. When she painted this lofty portrait, I became more infuriated than ever, and we'd get stuck in a repetitive, angry loop.

"So, Ma, if you loved Dad, and he was such a nice guy and you were 'happily married,' why did you have an affair?"

My mother stuck to her story: "The affair was harmless." "All marriages get boring." "You are young, and you don't understand." "What is it you want to know?"

Probably what I wanted to know was, What is the secret to a happy marriage? What sustains love? Her answer—that she had a happy marriage and had had an affair because she was "bored"—simply didn't compute for me.

This was a conversation that happened not once, but innumerable times. I'd begin with a bang and wind up feeling numb and foolish, estranged and scared. Although I, too, was married to a "difficult" guy—much more inflexible that I'd known when we'd married—I wanted to create a strong marriage. I had always sensed an uneasy disconnect between my mother and father. They were good parents and knew how to run a steady ship, but they seemed to lack the emotional closeness I yearned for. Starting in my adolescence, I'd vowed to create a close emotional connection when I married, and now, young and newly married, I wanted to hold on to my vision. I was certain that having an affair could create only distance, distrust, and trouble, even as my mother spoke in a way that seemed confident.

Over the years, whenever I looked back at this moment in my life, I would realize why I ended up feeling numb. My mother had been telling me that her behavior was justifiable in the face of frustration and boredom. I wasn't a person who was prone to feeling bored; nonetheless, in my marriage, I had already felt angry, resentful, and hopeless. Was having an affair the answer?

And she'd pulled me into a triangle. I, her daughter, was holding her secret about deceiving and betraying my dead father. She reminded me of Ellie, a woman in my college dorm my sophomore year of college, who bragged about "getting away with" cheating on her boyfriend. But this was not Ellie and her boyfriend; this was my mother cheating on my father. Her affair and her happiness about her affair were too much for me to deal with. She had habitually betrayed my father, and, I later realized, she had also betrayed me, her daughter. She had pulled me into the middle of her drama by asking me to keep her secret from my husband and my brother.

I should have said all of this to her, and I should have asked her why she had to tell me. I should have reminded her that I had just lost my father and was in mourning. I wish I had told her that *her* happiness about her affair, *her* comfort about betraying my father for eight years, brought *me* neither happiness nor comfort. In my opinion, that deceit was not an acceptable, justifiable pathway to happiness.

But I said none of those things. I don't really know why I had no voice. What I do remember is an unusually cold Tuesday evening in April. It was late for a snowstorm, but there I sat, at 2:00 a.m., rocking my baby and watching the flakes falling lightly, hearing the words, "It was harmless, dear." I thought I'd explode with frustration. But then I had an idea.

The next morning, I pulled out my phone book and called my babysitter, Andrea. To my delight, she had the morning free. Although it had snowed all night, now the sun was shining, the sky was a sparkling blue, and Andrea spontaneously offered to take Zach to the park. She arrived quickly. As soon as I'd bundled him up and we'd all waved goodbye, I pulled out the pile of graduate school applications I'd stacked neatly under my bed. They had sat there for more than a year. Ever since I'd been in high school, becoming a psychologist had intrigued me; later, when working as an English teacher in a school for emotionally disturbed kids, my appetite had been further whetted. At different times I'd toyed with returning to school, but the moment never seemed right. But now I was fired up. Within the week, I completed three applications for PhD programs in psychology. The following September, I returned to Fordham University to make sense of what I couldn't bear to think about but felt compelled to understand.

Steam

I remember the day I told my younger brother, John, about Lenny. John and I are four years apart, and we'd inhabited two different worlds growing up. I was the "boy-crazy daughter," and he was the "serious son," interested in politics, current events, and Judaism. As a teenager, I knew he was my father's favorite, and I was jealous of the closeness they shared, but by my mid-twenties, my father and I had bonded deeply. As I wondered how I was going to tell my brother about Lenny, my stomach churned.

John and I were standing in line in the Ferris Hall cafeteria at Columbia University, where he was studying for his PhD. My nose was filled with food smells, and I could see the steam rising from the silver heating trays of meatballs and mac and cheese, the two choices of the day. John had grabbed two plates from the tall stack, placing one on each of our trays, and I was following him down the cafeteria line, sliding my tray.

"Man, I'm hungry," he said. "For cafeteria food, the mac and cheese is edible, actually good. And it comes with a salad," he said, lifting his chin and pointing toward the salad bar on the far side of the cafeteria. Nothing looked appetizing to me, and I knew why. I dreaded seeing the look in his eyes when I told him, but I'd made a decision. I couldn't bear my aloneness.

"I have to tell you something as soon as we sit down," I said in a low voice. My hands were freezing.

He looked over at me. "What's wrong?" he asked.

I was silent.

"You look pale," he said.

I'd planned to tell him when we were settled down at a table and had some quiet and privacy, but something inside snapped. I think it was when our eyes connected. "Mom has a boyfriend."

How had I blurted it out? In my mind, I'd rehearsed breaking this news gently, but in that moment I couldn't access the delivery I'd prepared and practiced to myself. I couldn't help it. Although I hated to be the messenger, I probably felt a sense of relief. Carrying this huge secret had been a weighty burden.

I told him the whole story, blow by blow—that's my style, and I'm good on the details. I started with the day of her "confession" and wound up describing my trip out to Long Island. When I mentioned Lenny's name, my brother's eyes widened and his face dropped. He was in a state of understandable shock. I remember his response: "Do you think Dad knew?"

I told him I had no idea. I remember his second question, too. "Does Grandma Sophie know?"

Now, I see how protective my brother was of my father and our grandmother. She'd been a wreck ever since my father's diagnosis. "It's a *shanda* (a sham). A parent should never outlive a child," she had repeated, tearfully. The death of her son was one thing. How would she respond to the fact that her beloved daughter-in-law had been having an affair for eight years?

A Short, Short Tale

"*Did you hear about Peggy? Just weeks after Everett died, she's running around town with Lenny Nash.*"

"*Lenny? The overweight bald guy who sells insurance? Isn't he married?*"

"*Yup, he's married—or was married—to Elaine, the woman Peggy runs the PTA with. I hear Lenny and Peg have been together for years, and now he's divorcing poor Elaine.*"

"*But before we continue with Peggy, you know Judy is married to Arnie. A year after Judy and Arnie got married, Arnie's father ran off with his secretary. She's not too much older than Arnie.*"

"*Oh, my God, I heard about that—and did you hear what happened to Arnie's mother, poor thing? While she was playing cards, the movers came and cleared out the apartment. She came home to an empty apartment, with all the pictures gone from the walls and everything, including the piano, gone. He screwed her out of everything!*"

"*Arnie's father? Wasn't he an attorney?*"

"He was—that's how come he knew all the tricks."

"Wasn't she the one with the money? Hadn't she inherited it from her father?"

"She certainly was the one with the money—her family was in the real estate business. But lawyers—those guys know every loophole that exists."

———————

Four months after my father's funeral, on a warm spring day, Lenny left his wife. My mother and Lenny were out and about, the town gossips had a field day, and I was inundated with phone calls.

"What should I say, Ma? People are calling me, asking so many questions about you and Lenny."

"Use your own judgment, dear. I'm sure you'll handle this just fine. Just fine."

There they were, those maddening words of hers again. She was so confident about everything—that things would turn out fine, that whatever she or I did would be "just fine." I was so lost, distressed by her lack of concern. I'd been raised to think that the bonds of marriage were sacred, or at least important. All I could fathom was that I had been duped. I had to face it—maybe I was just too naive.

"And what does Grandma Lillian think about you and your Lenny, Ma?" I was praying my mother's mother, my grandmother, would be an ally and join in my outrage.

"Well, of course, she's so happy for me."

"Does she know that you and your Lenny were fooling around for the past eight years while Daddy was alive?"

"No, of course I didn't tell her all that. No need to—no need for me to get her upset with all those details. I really wouldn't want to upset her."

Thanks a lot, Ma. I should have said, "So nice that you didn't want to upset your mother, yet it was perfectly fine to upset me, your daughter." But I didn't. Only later would I ask myself, *Why didn't I say that?*

It's taken me a lifetime to answer that question. I could have challenged my mother, but perhaps my attachment to her trumped my distress. Perhaps after losing one parent, I was wary of losing the other. So my challenges went up in smoke. No answers that suited me, not then, not ever. She was impervious not only to emotional curiosity but to acknowledging her impact on me.

Several months later, on a hot August afternoon, we were sitting in the backyard of my parents' home. Zach was splashing in the plastic pool when my mother nonchalantly broached a delicate subject.

"Lenny's divorce is going to be final in a few months. And, dear, I'm thinking ... about the wedding ..." Her voice trailed off in that maddening way.

"Wedding?" I asked. I knew this was the plan, but between the plan and the event there was a big gap.

"Lenny and I were thinking how nice it would be if, instead of getting married in a restaurant ... how would you feel about us, after his divorce goes through ... maybe we can get married in your apartment?"

Now, looking back, I can see what happened. A cauldron of emotions must have bubbled up. My head must have been filled with voices screaming and yelling simultaneously: *Married in my apartment? Are you kidding? Champagne for the bride? No way!* As the cacophony of voices crescendoed to a dizzying pace and volume, a whiteout settled over me, blinding and deafening me to my own emotions. In the end, the voice of the good, dutiful daughter was the loudest.

"Sure, Ma. That would be fine."

For many years, when I looked back on this moment, I had trouble understanding why I'd agreed to host my mother's wedding. At first I saw myself as a compliant daughter who wanted to please my mother. After all, I had just lost my father, and perhaps I feared that putting my foot down would alienate her. Perhaps my lifelong fear of being abandoned, a residue from my childhood, never left me. Later, after studying theories of trauma, I expanded my lens on what could have accounted for my acquiescence. Our brains are structured to protect us from what we can't handle, and maybe, unable to process my own emotional reaction, I simply detached: I numbed out and shut down.

Six months later, immediately following the one-year anniversary of my father's death, my mom and Lenny tied the knot in my apartment. Lenny had gotten his divorce papers only days before the wedding ceremony. The divorce proceedings had become a huge hullabaloo, the details of which my mother (once again) inappropriately shared with me and I insanely listened to. To my mom's relief, the legal glitches, which included stories about Lenny's ex-wife's sleazy lawyer, calmed down before the big day.

I remember nothing about their wedding day. Maybe I was traumatized. PTSD may seem too dramatic a label for my reaction to something as ordinary—even mundane—as learning that my parents' marriage wasn't as loving and devoted as I'd imagined it to be and that in fact, my mother had been sleeping with Lenny for the past eight years. But losing my dad, and learning about my mother's lover, and holding the wedding at my apartment—it had to be too much. In retrospect, I wonder how I smiled while I poured the champagne.

I see from the photographs that I was physically present, but now I recognize that I was emotionally numb. I didn't yet know the word, but now I understand I coped by dissociating: I detached. In the one photo I framed, I am wearing a sexy turquoise dress with a stunning brass necklace. It's the only four-generation photograph I have from that era of my life. Zach, my eighteen-month-old son is in my arms. On one side of me is my mother's mother, Grandma Lillian, and on the other side is the glowing bride, my mother, resplendent in a beige eyelet dress drenched in sequins. My grandmother and my mother both wear wide smiles, and I am squinting, as if I have a headache. I wonder what I was trying to block when the photographer snapped that photo. Was I furious at my mother? Missing my father? Overwhelmed by what I imagined would be his shame if he were looking down?

Less than one year after their wedding, my phone rang at 2:00 a.m. It was my mother. She was in the Berkshires, alone in the house she and Lenny had bought. Lenny was dead. A massive heart attack had killed him instantly. She asked if I would come up.

PART THREE:

Becoming a Therapist

We all carry pain. Our muscles hold on to feelings and memories. Can you locate emotional pain or energy in particular areas of your body? Sadness? Anger? Hunger for connection? Breathe deeply into any of your hurt places. Inhale deeply, exhale completely. Nothing to do, nowhere to go—just notice what happens in your body when you breathe into the places where emotion seems to gather. Does the breath soften you? Or do those muscles tighten as you breathe? How does being with pain impact your body?

Jenny

It was 1979, I was thirty-seven years old, and it was my first day of my first job as a psychologist. After seven years of balancing diapers, a dissertation committee, two children, and a demanding husband, I had finished my PhD program and was finally a therapist. Eight-year-old Zach was in school all-day, four-year-old Rachel was off to nursery school, and I had found the perfect part-time job at a local clinic on Long Island, close to home. I'd vowed I'd never follow in my parents' footsteps and live on Long Island, but life has a way of changing us.

"You'll do great with the family I'm assigning you," Dr. Gunn, the clinic director, said warmly. A short, stout man, about my age, he had a warm smile that peeked through his trimmed mustache. He began by outlining the details of my first case, a recent referral he was turning over to me. "I spoke with the father, which is unusual," he said. "Usually it's the mothers who call. He's concerned about his fifteen-year-old daughter. He received a call from the guidance counselor at school that there's some kind of problem with this girl clamming up, avoiding others in the lunchroom. I know you don't have much experience doing therapy yet, but you were a high school teacher, so you're familiar with teenagers. Not many of us here have a great track record with teens. And this is a family that seems to be struggling with divorce—never easy for kids, but nothing life-threatening."

I shuddered. As a former high school English teacher, I loved working with teenagers, but as a teacher, I thought of myself more as an older sister or an adult friend/relative, not a wise therapist who was supposed to have expert listening skills that would draw out the inner workings of the mind. And I certainly qualified as having "not much experience." I had completed only a one-year internship doing psychotherapy, where every new patient had been a challenge.

And divorce? Dealing with a fifteen-year-old whose parents were splitting up felt daunting. These were waters I was terrified to swim in. Everywhere marriages were crumbling; women were becoming financially independent and leaving their husbands and sometimes even their children. I was deeply fearful that my own marriage might not survive this new phase of life.

While Arnie had been enthusiastic about my dream to become a psychologist and had supported, emotionally and financially, my going to graduate school to become a therapist, when I returned to school, we had only one child. And that was also before my interest in psychology had evolved into a consuming passion. Now, with two children to manage, one still a toddler, I knew our marriage was in trouble. Ever since I'd begun writing a dissertation and doing an internship, Arnie had become resentful, feeling neglected and irrelevant. For me, juggling the pressures of being a mother, wife, daughter, homemaker, and psychologist had become increasingly stressful, and my marriage often felt like a minefield, peppered with unexpected explosions from my husband and waves of my own resentment and grief.

And now my first new patient was dealing with divorce?

Two days later, dressed in my most professional blazer, I sat in my office awaiting the arrival of Jenny and her father, Walter. Both nervous and excited, I reread a chapter in *Family Theory in Clinical Practice*, a textbook by Murray Bowen, a pioneer in the field of family therapy. I had copied a list of questions Bowen suggested asking every family and tucked the list into the rear of my appointment book, hoping I'd have a chance to peek at my notes if I felt lost and needed a guide to our meeting. Little did I know how hard it would be to script a session when I was swept up in a family drama.

"Like I told you on the phone, Doctor, Jenny isn't talking much," Walter said as we began. His resemblance to his daughter was striking. Both were tall, thin, and lanky, with thick, wavy blond hair. Unaccustomed to being addressed as "Doctor," I tried to hide my awkwardness as Walter pursed his lips and spoke intensely. "She hardly talks to me," he continued in a low voice, "which is why I'm here today—maybe you can get her to talk." His voice sounded like it might crack. "She doesn't talk much to her mother, either, but Linda is hardly around these days. Most of the time, Jenny's in her room, with the door closed." Walter paused; his voice softened. "She's a great girl, my Jenny. But something's wrong. The phone hardly ever rings. And she doesn't laugh much anymore. It's hard to get her to crack a smile. Maybe it's because Linda moved out six months ago and we're getting divorced—as soon as the lawyers can get their act together. I think Jenny could be depressed."

"Thank you for bringing Jenny in," I said to Walter, after he gave me a few more details. "Now, please take a seat in the waiting room while I talk to her alone for a bit."

Hand on the doorknob, Walter turned back to me. "I forgot to mention something else. Jenny doesn't eat much either. I read something in the local papers about girls who don't eat. I think they called it anorexia nervosa. Ever heard of it?"

Droplets of sweat began to gather on my brow. A recent PhD, fresh out of graduate school, I had never heard anorexia nervosa mentioned in my seven years of graduate training. My professional credibility was on the line. Should I admit to being unfamiliar with the problems he might need help with?

As he stood waiting at the door, I racked my brain, wondering how to respond.

Suddenly, I heard my grandma Sophie's voice. I'd always loved how easily she paraphrased people she admired. One of her favorite, from Winston Churchill, popped into my mind: "There is a time in a person's life when he is tapped on the shoulder. It would be sad if he was unprepared or unwilling to do something that could lead to his finest hour."

"I don't really know much about anorexia," I told Jenny's father, "but I'm going to look into it."

As he closed my office door, I hoped my voice was sturdier than I felt inside. *Now what?* I wondered. *A girl who doesn't talk and has a problem I've never heard of?* My head was pounding.

"You heard me say I don't know much about anorexia," I said to Jenny, as I closed the door behind Walter. Looking her over carefully, I felt my stomach drop. I could see how frail she looked beneath her baggy sweat clothes. Her eyes bulged, and her face looked gaunt and sunken. I hoped admitting I knew nothing about anorexia hadn't made me seem like an idiot. "But I do know that people with anorexia starve themselves and are obsessed with losing weight. What about you? Are you having trouble eating?"

Jenny shrugged.

"Your shrug intrigues me," I said. "How old were you when you learned to shrug?"

Jenny shrugged again.

"Some people have a hard time with me," I said. "They think I ask a lot of stupid questions. They think I'm too nosy. So if you feel that way, let me know."

Jenny smiled.

"Are you the girl who doesn't eat and doesn't laugh?" I asked.

Jenny cracked a smile.

"No smiling here," I said.

The smile swept across her lips.

"When was the last time you laughed?"

Jenny began to cry. "I haven't been laughing much," she said, swinging her hair over her face.

I noticed her peeking over at me, but when our eyes met, she shrugged, tossed her thick blond curls back over her face, and looked away again. A memory of my teenage years emerged. How would I have felt being dragged to a therapist's office? How would I have survived if my parents had divorced and my mother had moved out?

"You haven't been laughing much since . . ."

"Since I gained weight."

To me, Jenny appeared to be a normal weight, but I decided not to challenge her. "When was it that you got so fat?"

"About six months ago," she said.

"Anything else happen then—six months ago?"

She shrugged.

"Here we go again with the shrugs," I said.

Jenny smiled.

"Six months ago—anything important happen if you look back?"

"Not that I can think of," Jenny said.

"Wasn't that when your mother moved out?" I asked.

Jenny shrugged again. "Maybe," she said, with another shrug and a yawn. "How would I know?" I hoped I hadn't scared her off.

"Maybe we should change the subject," I said, hoping to salvage our connection.

Jenny smiled and nodded. "What do you want to talk about?" she asked.

"What do *you* want to talk about?" I asked.

Jenny shrugged again and looked out the window.

"Okay," I said, "I'll go first. What do you think of me and my nosy questions?"

Jenny looked blank. I thought I'd hit a dead end, but she surprised me. "I think I'm fat, even though no one else agrees."

"Who's no one?"

"My friends. My parents. The school nurse. No one understands that I'm fat and I don't feel like eating."

"Oh, yeah," I said. "Now I remember. It was your guidance counselor who called the clinic. Your worried friends told her you'd been throwing away your lunch."

No response.

What now? I wondered. "Do you recall the time when you used to like to eat?" I asked.

No response, again.

I began to sweat. "Take a moment and think back to a year ago. What was your eating like then?"

Jenny had no trouble responding to me. "I was the girl who hung out at the mall and ate three slices of pizza for lunch or dinner." She had no idea exactly when or why her "old self" had vanished. But now she spent most of her time home alone, studying. Yes, she had lost some weight. No, she didn't know how much. Why didn't she eat? Because she wasn't hungry. Yes, she did feel fat, even though she was five foot five and weighed 110 pounds.

To my amazement, she agreed to come back for another session.

Before we ended, I invited her father to join us in my office. He was relieved to hear Jenny would return to see me. He'd been thinking about his own life while waiting. "I lost my mother to cancer when I was a little younger than Jenny," he said. "I probably never got over losing her. Do people ever really get over things?"

"You ask good questions," I said. "Unfortunately, most simple questions have complex answers. People can get over things. Can we talk more about this when we next meet?"

He nodded.

"I'd like to see you and your wife as soon as possible. Are you available next Tuesday night?"

I had no way of knowing that it would take three weeks for them to come in, and that by then Jenny would have lost two more pounds.

When the Student Is Ready

It's been said, "When the student is ready, the teacher appears." Jenny was my first teacher. The day after that first session with her, I remembered a conversation I'd had over the summer with an old friend, April, who had been talking about treating patients who wouldn't eat. That night, I called her.

"This is an epidemic," she told me. "We're starting a new study group at my institute—if you're free Wednesday afternoons, come join us."

By the following week, I'd changed my schedule and was traveling to the newly formed Center for the Study of Anorexia, a division of the Institute for Contemporary Psychotherapy in New York City. Within a month, I was assigned a few patients and was deeply immersed in learning as much as I could, quickly. Wednesday afternoons I saw patients, participated in a small study group, and met with an individual supervisor. As I began learning about how psychological stressors fed eating disorders, my fascination grew. The diet craze was sweeping the country—and so was the feminist movement. Was there a link? Everyone—including me and every female I knew—wanted to be thin. But risking death by not eating? I knew that twelfth- and thirteenth-century saints had starved themselves as part of a spiritual search, but I knew nothing about the current epidemic of starving teenagers, hell-bent on a relentless pursuit of thinness.

The center became my new professional home, filled with exciting colleagues and challenges. Within a couple of years, eating problems expanded to include bulimia, a brand-new diagnostic category. We now recognized a new breed of patients with eating disorders, who, instead of or in addition to starving themselves, had an arsenal of weapons to combat the fear of fat and all the emotional distress hiding beneath this obsession: vomiting, abusing laxatives, and exercising excessively. Our eating-disorder study group grew, expanded, changed its name, and became the Center for the Study of Anorexia and Bulimia. What I was most fascinated in understanding was how the fear of fat and the relentless pursuit of thinness both masked and expressed a host of deeper problems my patients were oblivious to. Focusing on something as concrete as food, weight, and calories allowed them to avoid feeling all kinds of complex experiences and painful issues. Inner pain that they could not acknowledge or speak about automatically translated into bingeing, purging, and starving.

Before long, my Long Island practice was flooded with patients, mostly teenage girls. Within a few years, I opened a center and began hiring and training therapists to work for me. There was no way during that initial meeting with Jenny and Walter I could have imagined I'd spend the next four decades working with patients with eating disorders and their families.

Two days after our first meeting, Jenny returned. Our session had begun to explore her fear of fat, which had appeared mysteriously and was now consuming her life. I felt certain that if I probed gently, she'd loosen up and reveal something more of her inner self.

"What can you tell me about your mom?" I asked.

"She's the greatest." Jenny started tapping her foot anxiously.

"I notice your foot—it's tapping away," I said, "I wonder if it has something to tell us."

Jenny smiled, shrugged, and was still.

"You didn't need to stop tapping," I said. "Your foot is talking to us, telling us something important that you might not have words for."

Jenny shrugged again.

"About your stopping tapping: I didn't want to make you feel criticized. Did you feel that way?"

"A little," Jenny said.

"I'm so glad you can tell me that," I said.

Jenny smiled.

"Talking about your feelings is what therapy is really all about. Sometimes we tap when we're nervous, and I wondered if you were nervous about anything."

Jenny shook her head no.

"Is it okay that I asked that question?" I said, and Jenny responded with a positive nod.

"We were talking about your mom," I said, not wanting to lose the opportunity to name what I assumed was an important part of her problem: the pain she must feel about her parents' divorce, her mother's move, and what I sensed must be feelings of abandonment and anxiety. "I don't want to be too pushy, but I know sometimes we all need a push. I'm wondering, how are you two getting along?"

"Really fine," she answered, quickly.

I took a deep breath. *Now what?* "Your dad mentioned she moved out. Where does she live?"

"In an apartment near the train station."

"How often do you get to see her?"

"Oh, she doesn't have much time for me since she moved out. I feel really bad for her. She has to get up really early to commute to New York City, where she has a big job in a busy advertising office. She has to work late so often that we don't really see much of each other during the week." *Tap, tap.* "But she comes over to our house for dinner when she can make it."

"What's it like not seeing much of her during the week?"

"I'm managing. Last night I made a brisket."

I noticed how Jenny had avoided answering my question, but decided it best to back off—for now. "So, you made a nice dinner for your mom. How considerate!" I said, thinking about how Jenny, who needed emotional nourishment, fed her mother but starved herself. "What was that like?"

"Oh, we didn't get to have dinner together." Jenny's face fell. Before I could say a word, she continued, smiling. "Her boss made her work late, so when she finished, she grabbed a bite with one of her friends in her office and I ate by myself," she said cheerily.

My heart sank. Here was a girl hungering for a connection with her mother, something I was familiar with. I had no idea that the hungry little girl inside me had decades of experience to help me connect with Jenny.

"I see," I said, picturing Jenny sitting alone at the kitchen table, probably barely touching her food. Therapy is a process of learning to access our emotional needs; for now, I wanted to help my starving Jenny not only honor those needs but take care of her most basic hunger: for food. "How was the brisket?" I asked, deliberately sidestepping the emotionally charged issue, her mother, fearful I'd alienate her. I knew from my work as an English teacher that kids become protective if they feel intruded upon. Sometimes starting with the concrete is the best way to reach deeper, internal issues, not only with a teenager but with anyone.

"Really good," she answered, and her foot tapping began again. She looked away, and I decided to ignore the tapping for the moment.

"Brisket can be rich," I said. "Were you able to eat much?"

"Not really," she said finally. "It was too fatty."

"You didn't eat the fatty parts, did you?" I asked, and in response, Jenny detailed how she cut off and discarded them. I imagined all that was left were a couple of tiny bites. However, not wanting to be too confrontational, I moved on. "When do you think you're going to see your mom next?"

She shrugged. "I never know. I'll just wait and see."

Regardless of how direct I was, Jenny revealed nothing of her feelings. When I inquired about her father, she gave a repeat performance. He worked at home but had long hours and she barely saw him. And he had a girlfriend now, Evvie.

I kept trying. "Evvie? You said you really liked her. What about her do you like?"

"Everything," she said flatly.

———

Three weeks later, I met with Jenny's parents. By now, in addition to seeing me, Jenny was seeing a medical doctor and a nutritionist regularly. Although she claimed to be eating exactly what her nutritionist suggested, she was still losing weight. I was witnessing exactly what I was learning in my training classes; a powerful unconscious need to lose weight was helping Jenny survive what she couldn't process emotionally. However, although her weight was dangerously low, since her heart rate, electrolytes, and other internal organ functions were normal, the doctor did not recommend hospitalization, although the possibility loomed.

Linda had canceled our first family therapy session, and Walter, the second. I understood that their schedules were crowded with professional commitments, but in the series of phone messages that surrounded the rescheduling, I got a dose of what I imagined Jenny suffered most of the time—feeling like an inconvenience and a burden.

"I don't want to be there when you meet with them," Jenny requested the day before the session. "They don't talk; they fight."

"What do they fight about?" I asked.

"Money. Who pays for what. Who pays for me and my stuff." Although I'd learned in graduate school it was generally best to see fifteen-year-olds with their parents, I made an exception. I knew that children do not benefit from witnessing parental fighting.

As it turned out, meeting Linda and Walter was a godsend and helped me understand Jenny. Both parents were fit, trim, and meticulously groomed. As with my mother, their outsides seemed more important than their insides.

Linda did most of the talking. She described their early life as "charmed." She and Walter met in high school and married after college graduation. Like my parents, Walter had joined his father's thriving family business, in lumber, and Linda, then an elementary school teacher, decorated their new home in her free time. The conception, pregnancy, birth, and infancy of their firstborn, Jenny's older brother, Jared, followed effortlessly. They were unprepared for what came next: two miscarriages and, when Jared was six, the death of their second child, just five days after her birth. She was buried nameless. Her death plunged Linda into the depths of desolation.

Tragedy, says a Chinese proverb, brings us to a crossroads where the fork of danger meets the fork of opportunity. It compels some people to turn to friends and family for support and comfort, while others withdraw. After the baby's death, neither Linda nor Walter could talk about their loss and sorrow. Instead, both became busier than ever. On a conscious level, neither of them wanted to burden the other. On a deeper level, neither could tolerate their feelings of grief. It was into this empty, devitalized world that Jenny was born, three years after the death of her unnamed sister.

Jenny was unplanned and born prematurely. For months after her cesarean section, Linda remained bedridden and depressed, while Jenny was cared for by a succession of nannies who complained about the colicky baby with feeding issues and cried continuously.

What was most striking about this tragedy was not the story, but the way it was told. Linda and Walter recounted the details of their family, including their divorce, without a trace of sadness. While both expressed concern about Jenny's weight loss, neither seemed struck by a sense of urgency or dismayed when I mentioned a potential hospitalization. I found it odd that her parents asked so few questions, so I began with a few of mine. When did they notice she'd stopped eating? Was she losing weight? Neither had much to say. What I understood was that they were as good at distancing themselves from their daughter's tragedy as they were at keeping away from their own. Jenny had learned well from them.

By now, I'd done some intense reading about eating dis-orders and realized the importance of including parents in the recovery process. Many parents were struggling with unre-solved pain from their own lives, and although they were committed to not repeating their parents' mistakes, they were bewildered about what constituted "good enough parenting." One mother expressed this common dilemma in this way: "How do I know what is right for my own daughter when I was parented so poorly myself?"

Trying to involve Jenny's parents in her care proved more challenging than I'd imagined.

"We live in a culture where thinness is overvalued," I began, wanting to educate them about how a seemingly normal behav-ior could spin out of control.

Neither parent seemed to get my message; both seemed eager to talk about their rigorous workout schedules.

"But everyone who wants to be thin doesn't develop an eating disorder," I continued, explaining that eating disorders are usually a way of coping with painful emotional feelings one is unable or unwilling to feel and express. "Sometimes it's easy to avoid our feelings by focusing on a distraction, and dieting can be a distraction—although when it's taken to an extreme, as in Jenny's situation, it can be life-threatening. You two seem to be handling your divorce well, but it may be more disturbing to Jenny than either she or you realize."

Clearly, her parents missed my point.

"Even though she's seen you a few weeks," her father said, "she's still worried about her weight. It's so silly, given how thin she is."

Because of this non sequitur, I wasn't sure he had heard me. And if he didn't listen to me, was he really able to listen to Jenny? "Telling her that her worries are 'silly' isn't going to help her feel close to or understood by you," I told her parents. "It will just frustrate her and won't keep her from dieting. Or worrying." I told them that a serious eating disorder takes a long time to develop and a long time to heal, and that in Jenny's case, part of the healing process would involve helping her feed herself, emotionally and nutritionally. "Being in her room by herself is a problem," I said, explaining that human connections are at the heart of healing and that isolation breeds problems. "It's important to help her feed herself—with food and by being with people who love her. You can help by being good listeners."

Linda and Walter nodded.

I had expected questions, but neither asked any, so I continued. "An eating disorder is always the tip of the iceberg—just a symptom, albeit a dangerous one, of an emotional problem. We have to ultimately address her dangerous symptoms, as well as the underlying issues. What will help your daughter most is your interest and presence in her life. Spend time with her. Find things you enjoy doing together that don't have to do with food, exercise, or dieting. When it comes to eating, if one of you can sit with her while she has breakfast and dinner, that would be great. Keep the nutritionist's suggestions handy, and ask her to follow the plan she's agreed to."

"Sounds good," Linda said.

Walter nodded.

"Is that a commitment?" I asked.

Linda's eyes glazed over.

Walter looked away.

"Can either of you make a commitment to sit with her while she eats dinner?"

"I cannot," Walter said firmly. "I'd love to be able to say yes, but I'm out of town a lot."

Linda seconded him. "My work schedule is unpredictable. I wish I were still teaching school, but in my new job, I'm out entertaining clients several nights a week," she said, a bit wistfully. "Unfortunately, it's impossible for me to always plan in advance."

Meeting with her parents gave me a new window into Jenny's life. After hearing they'd never sought therapy following their miscarriages, their stillborn child, or their divorce, I could see the tenacious wall surrounding their emotions. Like most of us, Jenny had absorbed her parents' essence. Like they were, she was estranged from her own emotional life.

Jenny's emotional estrangement was something I was keenly familiar with from dealing with my mother. Years of my own therapy had helped me face my helplessness at changing my mother's Pollyanna attitude and superficiality. In fact, I'd come to understand that these qualities served an important function: They protected her from facing unbearable emotions—her own or mine.

How, I wondered, would I ever break through the wall around Jenny?

Ben's Bagels

We'd been meeting regularly for several months, and Jenny's weight hovered just a pound or two above the weight at which her doctors would hospitalize her. I'd given her a journal, hoping she'd record her feelings, but, to my dismay, she filled it with lists of food, calories, and repetitive musings regarding her fear of eating and her dread about getting fat. Even my gentle questions were fruitless; getting reflective or deep seemed impossible for her.

The prevalent psychotherapy philosophy, "Let the patient lead," was guided by Freud's belief that insight was the royal road to change. I had been trained to be a passive, silent expert—a stance believed to allow hidden dilemmas to surface. But regardless of whether I remained silent or probed gently, Jenny remained clueless about any deeper motivation causing her fear of food, eating, or fatness. My anxiety mounted as she failed to eat or gain weight and I witnessed her anorexia become more deeply entrenched.

Eventually, it dawned on me. Maybe I should switch my approach.

"Are you willing to do an experiment?" I asked her one day. I ignored her shrug. "Maybe we could eat something together. Are you willing? We could share something small, like an apple."

Reluctantly, she agreed.

I remember how daring I felt when I first brought that apple to my office. I decided to keep my plan to myself, rather than risk criticism from a supervisor or colleague.

At our next session, both Jenny and I were amazed; she picked up the first slice and ate it. A second slice, and then a third followed. Within moments, half of the slices on her plate had disappeared.

"How was it?" I asked.

"Delicious!"

"What a risk you took!" I said. "I'm impressed."

She beamed. *Green light*, I told myself. *We're entering new territory.*

"Did you know you could be such a risk taker?" I asked.

She shrugged; she didn't think of herself in that way. She wasn't sure why she had stopped eating apples or why it was so easy to eat one in my office.

"Well," I said, "often we don't know why we do things." By now, I was learning that recovery from anorexia often occurs without any insight into the origin of the illness. "I'm guessing you've noticed eating the apple really impresses me and makes me happy, too," I said. "I felt it was risky of me to bring this apple here. I didn't want to be pushy—I didn't want you to be frustrated or fail. But something inside me wanted to take this risk with you." Jenny said nothing, so I continued. "Perhaps there are other risks we might take," hopefully, deep within her brain, planting a seed that change was possible. "I'm really impressed with you," I repeated.

She shrugged, but I noticed she was smiling.

"What's it like to hear how impressed I am?" I asked.

Jenny smiled again and sat silently, but I didn't want to let go of a precious opportunity to talk about our relationship. Maybe if I modeled my own vulnerability, she would, too.

"I wonder if you know it's unusual for me to suggest we eat together."

Jenny shrugged but looked curious.

"I told you I ask a lot of nosy questions," I said. "Maybe you have some questions for me?"

She didn't. But sharing an apple would become our ritual and would open up endless conversations about the fruit, the process of change, and our relationship.

A couple of sessions later, I was in for another surprise. Jenny sat down, and when I passed her the apple slices, she asked, "Do you eat with your other patients?" A bit of probing opened up new vistas. What she really wanted to know was if she was special to me. She also shared a worry about me. "If you eat with all your patients, you're going to get fat!" she said.

"I don't think eating half an apple a couple of times a day is going to make me fat," I said. "But maybe you want to know how I'd feel if I gained weight?"

She nodded.

"Well, I don't really want to gain a lot of weight," I said. I told her I saved my worrying for other things.

"Like what?" she asked.

"Like whether I'm getting through to you," I told her. "Am I?"

Before long, we were talking about our relationship, and talking about our relationship opened up new doors.

Another surprise awaited me.

"Do you exercise?" she asked one day.

"I'm wondering why you're asking me," I responded.

Jenny looked away.

Oh, no—red light, I thought, realizing I'd missed an opportunity to encourage her curiosity about me and maybe get closer. "I love to play tennis and ride my bike," I told her. "I try to exercise a couple of times a week. I guess I should have told you that before I asked you that question, right?"

Jenny looked over at me and nodded. "My parents exercise every day," she said. "They're afraid of getting fat."

"Wow," I said, hoping she'd say more, but she didn't. I decided to focus back on us. "I'm wondering if you worry about eating an apple with me."

Jenny nodded. She did.

"Eating an apple isn't going to make you fat," I said. "What else are you worrying about?"

To my surprise, she responded with a question that contained profound implications for our relationship. "Do you ever get bored eating apples with me?" she asked.

"A little bored with the apples," I said. "Not with you. What about you?"

"I'm getting bored with apples," she confessed. "Can we try something else?"

I was astounded. "Any ideas?" I asked.

"Do you know the bagel store around the corner? They have the best onion bagels! Ever since I've been coming to your office, I've been dreaming about them. I used to love going there with my mom when I was little."

I still remember how nervous I was leaving my office and walking to the bagel store. I felt like I had violated the basic rules of Good Therapy 101. Weren't therapists supposed to help patients become reflective and develop insight, rather than take neighborhood excursions?

Sitting at a small table in the rear, we shared an onion bagel with light butter.

"I see a frown," I said. "Are you worrying about eating this bagel?"

She wasn't.

"Anything else on your mind?" I asked.

"I'm wondering why some of my best friends dropped me."

"Dropped you? How upsetting," I said. "What's happening?"

Her story about being bullied by the thinnest girl in her class, who had once been her best friend, dribbled out.

"Relationships are never easy," I said.

She was so busy talking that she hadn't finished her half of the bagel when it was time to leave. "Can I take it back to your office with me?" she asked.

"Of course," I said.

She packed it up happily.

"What did you think of our excursion?" I asked when we were back in my office.

Jenny smiled. "Can we go back there again?"

Jenny was my first patient with an eating disorder. The work I did with her would come to define me as a therapist, fueling a passion that became my lifelong professional focus: treating people with eating disorders. Although the idea of trying to help a starving fifteen-year-old on the brink of hospitalization was daunting to a beginning therapist, I leaped in. At the time, I attributed my fearless enthusiasm to my previous experience as a high school English teacher—I had honed my skills at creating bridges to unreachable teenagers.

But something rare had happened between Jenny and me. We had come together at a critical time for each of us. She was lost, isolated, and in danger. I reached out to her, fumbling my way with patience and gentle persistence. Although at that time I was unaware, I now understand that connecting to her pain helped me connect to my own. Giving her the attention and respect for her feelings that I had always longed for from my own mother was healing for me. Since little was known about how to reach patients with eating disorders back then, I was free to be creative, unburdened by clinical protocols. I couldn't have known that leaving my office and taking this walk with her would be the beginning of a breakthrough for me, as well as for her. Jenny inspired me to take a risk and veer off the traditional therapy path; only now do I wonder if she absorbed my stretching and was inspired to follow my lead and take her own risks.

While I knew nothing about eating disorders and my parents hadn't divorced, I knew a lot about feeling abandoned by an emotionally remote mother. Reaching out to her was a way I nourished not only her but myself as well. The intimacy Jenny and I forged together filled a deep void in each of us.

Alyssa

It was a late afternoon, the Friday before Memorial Day weekend, when I received an unusual voicemail.

"Hi, Dr. Rabinor. My name is Alyssa, and I'm home from my junior year of college and leaving in five weeks for a summer program in Massachusetts. I'd like to come in for a checkup; please call me back as soon as possible," she said, before leaving her phone number.

The timing of the call raised my suspicions. Many people approach a first session with a new therapist ambivalently; the timing of this call, just before a long holiday weekend, was a red flag. I would have to keep my antennae up. On the one hand, this new patient had called, wanting help. On the other hand, she had created a situation in which I was unlikely to return her call for several days.

When we finally spoke on the phone the following Tuesday, she introduced herself as a "recovered binge eater" and repeated her unusual request, asking if she could have a checkup before she left for Cambridge to attend summer school.

A petite woman with short, curly blond hair arrived in my office a week later, clad in baggy jeans and an oversize blue work shirt, the common garb of my patients with eating disorders, who generally either wished to hide their bodies to mask their emaciation or feared being seen as overweight. I began our work with the age-old questions: What exactly was happening, and why was she seeking a checkup now?

Well spoken, Alyssa expressed her distress. Recent "fat attacks" had appeared from out of nowhere. She assured me she was neither starving nor bingeing nor vomiting, yet she could not stop ruminating about "feeling fat," even though she knew her weight was in the normal range. Her obsessive preoccupation about what to eat, when to eat, and her weight unnerved her. She described herself as a "gym rat" with an array of concerning symptoms—some days she weighed herself a dozen times or more, she was continuously computing her calories in a notebook she carried with her twenty-four-seven, and she was phobic about mirrors. Her fear of fat was interrupting her life, big time. She was afraid she was relapsing and being pulled back into her eating disorder, and, if so, she wanted to understand what was happening to her.

While obsessing about food, weight, and body image was and is so prevalent in Western culture that it hardly seems abnormal, the symptom picture she was reporting was outside normal behavior. I was reassured to hear she was worried. Obsessing about food and weight are compelling distractions, but what could have been bothering her so much that she needed a distraction?

As she spoke about her current life, I began to formulate questions. Was she feeling anxious about the upcoming summer session at the prestigious, high-pressure university? Was she worried about her plans after graduation, only a year away? She had confided how ill prepared she felt as an English major to enter the workforce. She felt pressure from her parents, both attorneys, to apply to law school, which had once been her dream, but now she was not excited to attend. And then there was her boyfriend, Ned, another issue. Ned had graduated, gone into his family's business, and wanted

Alyssa to move in with him after graduation. She was not sure she could face that decision. She didn't want to lose him, but after three years of being together, Ned was itching for a commitment.

Her life was woven tight with many threads to unravel. We agreed to meet for weekly sessions until her departure, on July 1.

Our next two sessions flew by. We went back and forth between examining her present concerns and exploring the origins of her binge eating. She had vivid memories of how it had started. She'd been in her junior year of high school when, the day after her sweet-sixteen party, her entire group of girlfriends had dropped her. She had no idea why, but not one friend had called her the Sunday after the party. When she arrived at school that Monday morning, she was friendless. No one was speaking to her.

Initially, Alyssa was dismissive of how being shunned might have impacted her, but, knowing that being bullied is traumatic, I encouraged her to dig deep. To her surprise, as she talked about that unhappy period in her life, buried pain, heretofore minimized, emerged.

"Whom did you turn to for support?" I asked, and her eyes filled with tears.

"I had no one," she said softly, recalling what it was like to ride on the school bus, the only person sitting alone in a seat designated for two.

"Take a deep breath and see yourself on the bus," I suggested, hoping reaching into her pain would be the first step in letting go of it. "It's not necessary to say more than you want—just breathe deeply and be with whatever comes up." I was hopeful that getting in touch with her long repressed pain might help her feel less alone and help her develop some self-compassion.

Alyssa began to cry. "I can't talk about it," she said. "It was so awful."

"Being shunned *is* awful," I said, after a moment, and more of her agony—and shame—tumbled out. "And your parents? How did they react?" I asked.

Her response didn't surprise me. She hadn't told them—shame had gotten in her way. I wondered if the isolation she had to deal with was as traumatic as being scapegoated and abandoned by her friends. As she spoke, she began to understand how overeating and then starving had been her way of coping with what was inexpressible: her rejection, isolation, and shame.

"You really zeroed in on the scapegoat incident," she said, as she was standing at the door, ready to leave our fourth session. "I never realized how alone I felt, ashamed to talk about my feelings with anyone, even my mother. How were you able to know how I'd suffered?"

Her question caught me off guard. I had another patient sitting in the waiting room, but that wasn't the only reason I felt a sense of pressure and unease. I knew why I'd been so attuned to her trauma; our own pain is often a window on others' suffering. Sitting with Alyssa week after week had evoked my own memories of being bullied when I was in junior high school.

I was unsure how to respond. Self-disclosure of personal information by therapists is a controversial topic today, and two decades ago, when I saw Alyssa, it was frowned upon, if not disparaged. Therapists who volunteer personal information were and are still often characterized as possessing poor judgment and described pejoratively as having "loose boundaries." I'd been initially trained to keep my personal life experience out of my office, but something inside me was moved when Alyssa asked me that question. I knew that feeling isolated was at the root of an eating disorder, and I felt an urge to undo her aloneness.

"I had a similar experience in my last year of junior high school," I said. "And to this day, I've never understood how I became the target of the meanest girl in my seventh-grade class."

Alyssa's eyes widened.

"Listening to your experience reminded me of all that happened that awful year. I remember being terrified to go to school each day. You might have thought that decades later, I would have forgotten about it," I said, "but not so. Let me tell you a story."

I'd recently attended the theater and was sitting in the balcony, when, just before the curtain rose, I looked down into the orchestra below. To my surprise, I spied my old junior high school tormenter. There she was—the ringleader of the vicious pack of mean girls. Suddenly, she looked up at the balcony and spotted me. Our eyes met, she waved, and as I automatically raised my hand and waved back, my stomach dropped and I felt a forty-year old wound burst open. The house lights went down, the play started, but I was unable to concentrate on the theatrical performance on the stage. Instead, I was lost in my own drama. Memories of that miserable year in my life bubbled up. I summarized my experience: "I felt nervous, powerless, scared, bitter, and vengeful—all at the same time."

"Oh my goodness," Alyssa said.

"I couldn't believe that those old emotions were still raw," I told her. "I guess that's how I understood your pain. Painful experiences that are silenced stay with us a long time; they live on, buried in our bodies."

Alyssa stared at me, wide-eyed and immobilized. "Thank you for telling me all this," she said, before she walked out of my office, smiling.

Alone in my office, I found myself thinking about our session. My inner critic was activated as I wondered how this personal information about me would impact Alyssa. Would she feel closer to me, or had I pushed her away? My mind raced. First, I felt ashamed about having disclosed my pain. Would she think of me with pity? Would she think of me as a loser? Next, had I overstepped a professional line and violated one of the basic rules of good psychotherapy?

After reminding myself to take three deep breaths, I began to feel a bit more assured. I realized I had intuitively acted from a solid position, attempting to validate Alyssa's situation by being emotionally vulnerable and authentic. And as my breathing calmed down, I found that my mind had wandered back to that miserable year of junior high school, to the dread that accompanied me as I got up in the morning, brushed my teeth, left home, and walked through the schoolyard gates, seeing the pack of girls awaiting me with tormenting barbs. In my imagination, I could feel the glaring eyes of the ringleader piercing me as her sarcastic jeers left me raw.

I felt a pit growing in my stomach. Why did this incident continue to bother me? I thought I had finished processing this experience in my personal work on myself, yet something clearly remained unfinished. Sitting in my office, I realized something new: the pain of seventh grade wasn't only about being rejected by the mean girls. It was also about feeling isolated by and disconnected from my mother. As I stayed in this space, another memory emerged.

I was twelve years old, sprawled across my bed, crying. I'd raced home from school, feeling miserable—helpless, hopeless, and friendless. My mother came into my room. She sat down beside me on my bed, put her arms around me, and in a firm voice said, "Just stop crying now, dear. You won't even remember these mean girls a few years from now."

"She was my best friend," I wailed, thinking about the ringleader, as my sobs increased. My mother hugged me more tightly.

"This really isn't such a big deal!" she said. "No more crying, Judy. And if you think losing your best friend hurts, just wait until you lose a boyfriend." A detailed narrative followed as my mother described her heartbreak when her first boyfriend dropped her.

At the time, I remembered my head was pounding as she spoke, and I felt nauseous. Didn't my mother understand how much I hurt? How was I supposed to let go of what hurt so badly? Didn't she understand how much I would like to—but couldn't—let go of my feelings? Was there something wrong with me that I was suffering so much and making a big deal about something unimportant?

Lessons on Listening

The following session, Alyssa arrived a few minutes late. She began with an apology, but within moments, a tear trickled down her cheek.

"Dr. R., I've lied to you—or at least I haven't been one hundred percent truthful." She paused to catch her breath. "There's something I haven't been able to tell you—or anyone. I've been harboring a secret: I've been vomiting for over a year. I told everyone I was having 'fat attacks,' but there's more. I've been throwing up—not every day, just once in a while, but since I've been home, the vomiting has gotten worse. I'm frightened, and no one knows. I haven't even told Ned. And now I'm leaving for Cambridge for the rest of the summer, and I'm really scared. What should I do?"

"Thank you for trusting me," I said, and she burst into tears. "Your tears—what are they saying?"

"I feel so much better being able to be honest with you," she said, and we proceeded to process what it had been like for her to have sat silently in my office with her secret. One part of her, she realized, had longed to be truthful, but another part of her was silenced by years of buried shame and the habitual isolation it breeds. "Keeping things to myself is a bad habit," she said.

"The good thing about habits," I told her, "is that we can break old ones and create new ones." I asked if she knew what had allowed her to open up, and she smiled. "Your story pushed me to be truthful. I needed it. Thank you." Before she left, we arranged for a series of phone sessions when she got to Cambridge, so we could continue to address the next chapter of her healing.

Several years later, when I was writing a chapter about the impact of therapists' self-disclosure on patients, I contacted Alyssa and requested permission to tell our story. In response, she wrote me the following letter (and since then has given me permission to reprint it here):

> Dear Dr. R.,
> Thank you for sending me your chapter. Reading it made me think about all I've learned in my psychology class this semester. I know that many professionals frown upon a therapist revealing parts of their life to a patient. However, I think that by allowing the patient into your life, you set up a much more comfortable situation for the patient. . . . The first psychologist that I went to, before I saw you, made me very uncomfortable. In fact, I dreaded going to her office once a week. I always felt like she was judging me, looking at me as just a patient with a problem, rather than as a real person. There is much more to my life than just the eating disorder, but none of that concerned her. She was also very secretive about herself. I didn't know anything about her, and so I was uncomfortable revealing so much to someone whom I didn't know anything about. Most things in life are give and take, and I think I was uncomfortable in giving away so much private information about myself and not really receiving anything in return . . . I didn't want her

life story; I just wanted for her to maybe relate something that I was saying to an experience of her own. I wanted to be treated like a real person with real emotions, but instead I felt like this object she was trying to analyze and fix.

Your technique is very different from hers, but when I first started seeing you, I definitely didn't realize that my relationship with you was going to be so different from mine with the other therapist. You do not demand information, and you do not set up a wall dividing yourself from your patients. As a result, I felt much more comfortable confiding in you and asking for help. I realized it wasn't about being judged, analyzed, and, as a result, cured. Basically, from our first session together you assured me that therapy was a lengthy process, and that there was no timeline or calendar that we were trying to adhere to. Knowing that you weren't expecting instant results from me took off so much of the pressure and allowed me to be honest with you each session, instead of beating around the bush or just lying.

Alyssa's letter reminded me of lessons I've learned in my office, lessons that have helped me grow into a better listener in every relationship—as a parent, wife, friend, and supervisor. While psychotherapy is often called the "talking" cure, a better way of thinking about it is as the "listening" cure. The therapist's job is to help patients learn to listen deeply to themselves, with curiosity. How to create this environment is what makes psychotherapy more of an art than a science. By being attuned listeners, therapists are role models. An old professor of mine who lectured on the creative aspect of being a therapist repeatedly stressed that there are no formulas. Therapists find their own style, he insisted: "Different strokes for different folks." While I have always been an avid reader and loved attending seminars and workshops, I'm quite certain that our own dynamics are what most profoundly determine and shape the ways in which we develop our therapeutic stance. Certainly, my own experience growing up left me yearning for a strong, palpable listening presence, and undoubtedly, I offered Alyssa what I needed most myself.

What I knew intuitively from my own life experience was that sharing pain with my friends generally led them to be more open and honest about their troubles. What I learned early on was a basic tenet of connecting with anyone: Self-disclosure promotes self-disclosure. Perhaps, as Alyssa pointed out, the blank-screen therapeutic stance often creates an off-putting imbalance that actually impedes patients from being vulnerable. It is easy to minimize the power that comes from simply being a fellow traveler—a genuine, brave, wounded healer. Although we never know exactly why healing occurs, perhaps my authentic disclosure was the nudge Alyssa needed to be vulnerable, truthful, and courageous enough to begin the next leg of therapy and her own growth.

PART FOUR:

Love, Marriage, and Divorce

Imagine it is a holiday before you were born: Thanksgiving, New Year's Day, Christmas, Passover, or the Fourth of July. Imagine your mother sitting at the holiday table, pregnant with you. How does she feel about her pregnancy? Who is at the table with her? Who is missing? Take a moment to breathe into this image. Feel that primordial connection to her, that connection that defies language.

Ella

After working in the field of eating disorders for fifteen years, I switched my focus. By my early fifties, my practice was filled with adult binge eaters, who, unless they were morbidly obese, generally posed fewer medical worries than anorexic and bulimic teens. Nor did they present the cumbersome scheduling problems always involved in arranging family sessions with adolescents. So when Ella, my forty-seven-year-old patient, swept into my office that windy November morning, I wasn't prepared for the roller coaster ride I was about to take.

Elegantly dressed in a long black wool coat with a lush fur collar, Ella, a tall, broad-shouldered woman with curly auburn hair began talking before she even sat down. "I've come to a decision," she said, plopping onto my couch. "I'm getting divorced. I'm leaving Al when Jeremy goes to college next September."

She'd been complaining about her husband since our first session, so I wasn't surprised.

"Ella, we have a lot of work to do this year before you make the biggest mistake of your life."

Ella gasped. So did I.

It took me a moment to realize what I'd said. I'd meant to tell her, "We have a lot of work to do before you make the biggest *decision* of your life." How had I committed such a blunder?

A year earlier, Ella had walked into my office, concerned with her weight.

"I know why I'm overweight—I eat too much. What I don't understand is why I can't stop eating, and why I'm so out of control."

Although I was familiar with her complaint, I was intrigued. Eating too much—or too little—is always a story of pain. In response to my invitation, "Tell me about your weight problem," Ella slouched down into her chair, and her story unfolded. Every day, she awoke with a firm dedication to healthy eating. Her commitment usually held out until evening, but by nine or ten o'clock at night, the call of the kitchen inevitably overrode her determination to lose weight. The shelf above the microwave held her longings: M&M's, peanut butter–filled pretzels, Tate's coconut cookies—she couldn't resist.

"Imagine a world with no M&M's, peanut butter–filled pretzels, or Tate's cookies," I suggested, after we did a short relaxation. Before long we were addressing her inner hungers.

As I shifted our focus to her internal world, instead of her weight, her connection to herself deepened. "I appear to be a woman who has everything, but I'm empty inside," she said soulfully. A successful husband, three daughters who had graduated from college and were launched, a son who would soon be entering a prestigious university—Ella knew she had much to be grateful for. But all the trimmings of the good life—Broadway theater, fine restaurants, and luxurious family holidays to Maui and Aspen—did not satisfy her inner hungers. She felt lonely, isolated, and ashamed to admit her feelings. Instead of honoring her emotional needs, she took refuge in eating and distracted herself from her internal pain.

To her surprise, talking about her eating and her feelings helped her think about her hungers, for food and more. We began meeting twice weekly, and her bingeing decreased. Unfortunately, a sense of painful disconnection from her husband, Al, came into focus. A CEO and self-proclaimed workaholic, Al functioned at home the way he did in his marketing firm—as a dominating, controlling boss. Late business dinners kept him out most evenings when he wasn't traveling across the globe. In our sessions, Ella began to realize it was the emotional, not the geographical, distance between them that troubled her. She worked hard to open up a more intimate connection with Al, and she pushed him into agreeing to try couples therapy.

"You two are going to have to learn to live with and respect your differences or separate," their therapist told them firmly after only a few meetings, when it became clear that Al was not interested in "wasting time" in therapy.

"He's the second couples therapist who has given up on us," Ella said, tears in her eyes. "Maybe we're hopeless."

Coming to grips with their inability to benefit from couples therapy had ushered in a new wave of gloom for Ella—a despair I was familiar with. My own track record in marital therapy with Arnie had been unsuccessful, and, after several years of struggling with our marriage, my husband and I had divorced. Not until years afterward was I able to appreciate that the breakup of a marriage is the disintegration of an entire universe of extended family ties, social networks, and rituals that ground life. Not until later did I have a perspective on what it means to lose a partner with whom to make and share family history. Not until then was I aware that I'd been oblivious to the many long-term losses that are inevitable consequences when a marriage dies.

———

When she had arrived at my office that windy November morning, ready to leave her miserable marriage, Ella had expected to hear my congratulations. Instead, I'd given her a dire warning.

"You think divorcing Al is making the biggest mistake of my life?"

Trying to recover my balance, I remained silent for a moment. I shook my head. "I'm not sure what I think," I said sheepishly. "But I have to admit it's what I said."

"Maybe you just made a Freudian slip?" Ella asked.

"Maybe," I said, stalling for time. My head began to pound.

"Let me tell you what happened this weekend," Ella said. As she began to catalog Al's unacceptable deeds—his lateness for Jeremy's birthday dinner, barking at her in front of the family—a red flag went up in my mind.

"I need to interrupt you for a moment," I said, not wanting Al's bad behaviors to overshadow what had happened between us.

Freudian slips are important. They often reveal unconscious thoughts and feelings that may feel too dangerous to articulate. What was the meaning behind my slip? I was under the microscope, wishing I could escape. Escape, however, was not really an option. Exploring what lay beneath my words was my responsibility.

"You are correct—I made a slip. It's important *we* think about it," I said, intentionally stressing the "we." I imagined it had implications for both of us.

"No big deal," Ella said, shrugging off my comment. "To me, you made an innocent mistake. One thing's for sure—I don't want to forget to tell you how out of control I was last night. The leftover Chinese food Jessie had ordered in got me in trouble this time. I don't even like spare ribs, but I ate at least eight or ten cold ones *and* the shrimp fried rice, too. What bothered me was that even as I was eating, I knew I wasn't hungry. I haven't binged like this in ages."

Although Ella had confidently expressed her hunger for divorce, the cold spare ribs signaled trouble. I wondered if her "decision to divorce" had triggered this binge. Ella seemed more than willing to sweep away my "innocent mistake," but I imagined it had impacted her. If she felt criticized by me, our relationship—and her healing—were both in jeopardy. Suddenly, as I sat with her, a memory arose in me.

I was forty years old, recently separated from my husband. This was our first Thanksgiving apart in fifteen years, and I was driving my children from Long Island to my brother's wife's family home in Boston for the holiday weekend. A light snow was falling steadily, and the icy road terrified me. At that moment, it dawned on me: My ex-husband, who loved driving (which I hated), would have been at the wheel in this snowstorm if we had been together. Marriage had sheltered me from all kinds of anxieties, snowy roads being the least of them.

As I was digesting this sobering thought, thirteen-year-old Zachary piped up from the backseat. "Mom, why do we have to go to Boston?"

"Yeah, Ma, why?" nine-year-old Rachel chimed in.

"Because we're going to be with our family, with all your cousins." I tried to sound cheerful, although by then I had realized it wasn't just the icy roads I dreaded.

"Our *family*?" Zach asked. His voice dropped. "Ma, where's Dad going to be today? Whose house is he going to be at?"

As Ella and I sat in the silence, I fought back tears gathering behind my eyes. Perhaps the pain of my own divorce had triggered my "slip." Maybe my own experience was relevant to Ella. Where was the line between my experience and hers? Eventually, I felt an inner shift. "Are you willing to try an experiment?" I asked.

Ella nodded.

"Close your eyes, and breathe deeply," I said, as I lowered my voice and spoke slowly to help her quiet down and go inward, hoping to give her access to the concerns and fears that might be buried beneath the spare ribs.

"Imagine it's a year from now. You and Al are divorced. It's the week before Thanksgiving. The kids are all coming home from college in a few days, and you're planning the holiday meal. Where will you be living? Where will Al be living? And the kids—are they coming back to your house? To Al's? And think about Al—is he alone? Does he have a girlfriend? A woman with whom he will share the holidays?" I paused, wanting Ella to absorb all she might have to contend with. "And after Thanksgiving comes Christmas. Think about trimming the tree."

I stopped talking, wanting to give Ella time to ponder. She quickly opened her eyes.

"What came up for you?" I asked.

Tears trickled down each of her cheeks. "I never thought about any of this," she said. "Just thinking about the children—how disappointed they would be without Al at the Thanksgiving table. It sounds stupid, but who would carve the turkey? That's Al's job! And when you mentioned trimming the tree without him, that was so upsetting. I don't want to be married to him, but thinking about the holidays without him . . . the picture that came up wasn't what I expected."

I could hear my heart pounding. "It wasn't what I expected" echoed my experience that snowy Thanksgiving long ago—and how we both felt about my Freudian slip.

Ella was breathing heavily, her face flushed. She was visibly upset. "You've brought up a lot. You've made me think about so many things I hadn't thought about," she said.

"Let's bookmark dealing with 'the unexpected' for our next session," I said, as our meeting was coming to a close.

Ella stood up. "One last thing," she said at the door. "Let's put the spare ribs on next week's agenda, too. And my weight. I must have gained two pounds last night."

Ella's parting words didn't surprise me. It's easier to think about the damage of a spare-ribs binge than to ponder the realities of divorce. It's easier to be dismayed about gaining two pounds than to imagine grieving a failed marriage. I wondered how Ella would deal with all that had come up in our session.

Ella was my last patient of the day. After she left my office, I leaned back in the plush brown leather chair I'd been sitting in for the past twenty years. My mother had generously bought it for me when, at thirty-seven years old, I opened my first psychotherapy office and started a private practice.

"My treat," she insisted, when we spotted it in Bloomingdale's.

"It's ridiculously expensive. I don't need this kind of chair, Ma."

"I know you don't need it, but just sit in it and you'll see," she insisted.

I sank into the soft leather. She was right—it was delicious. "Feels great." I beamed.

"This chair is made for you—and you deserve it. After all that hard work and the years of studying! A real therapist's chair for the therapist!" she said proudly.

As I sat now in the quiet, my thoughts went back to Ella. As I've already elaborated, I was trained in the era of the "blank screen"—I was taught to keep my personal opinions and life experiences out of the therapy office. Therapists, I was told, are powerful authority figures with parent-like qualities who are not supposed to give advice or influence patients, but my own saga of divorce, dating, and single parenting had been vividly resurrected and had informed my thinking.

Painful memories from my thirteen years between marriages were easy to access: the challenge of single-parenting two children, especially when one was ill, and my loneliness on weekends when the kids were with Arnie—to say nothing of managing my own finances. I recalled how, when an unexpected oil-burner breakdown had brought on a financial crisis, I had found myself packing my schedule with new patients to offset staggering and unexpected bills. And the years of dating? At first I had felt like a gleeful teenager on a high, but the infatuation of new love was inevitably short lived, and the aftermath—being disappointed or depressed—hard to bear. Throughout, there had been the relentless fear that I would never meet Mr. Right and would be forever single.

Although I respected and understood Ella's dismay at being in a marriage that didn't work, I'd felt compelled to warn her about the problems divorce would inevitably bring. Now, though, new questions nagged: Was my personal experience relevant to Ella? Did I have a responsibility to warn her of the bumpy road ahead?

Leaning back in my therapist's chair, I thought about a conversation I'd had with my mother when I was on the brink of divorce.

It was a hot and humid afternoon, late August, two years after I had expanded my garage, built a home office, and opened my private practice, when I climbed into my blue Catalina Pontiac, left my home in Lido Beach, Long Island, and drove to my mother's York Avenue apartment in New York City. Sweating, I arrived, ready to break the news. I had been married for fourteen years, and Arnie and I had drifted apart. I was lonely, frustrated, and tired of trying to make our marriage work, and so was he. I was thirty-nine years old, frightened, and filled with despair on the one hand and hope on the other.

As my mother and I sat on her chintz couch, sipping chardonnay, I said, "Arnie is out of control, Ma. He's always angry with me—it's one thing after another. This time, it was my flight from San Francisco Sunday night—it was delayed, and I got home very late. Arnie was furious at me, as if it were my fault."

My mom stared at me blankly. Had she forgotten I'd been in San Francisco? I was proud of having been a keynote speaker, but perhaps it hadn't registered with her. Once again, I felt dropped by her, just as I had when she had been too busy to attend my PhD graduation. Just like a million little moments when I felt she wasn't really listening.

My stomach was cramping, but I plowed on.

"I'm done, Ma. Arnie wants a wife from the '50s—not me. If I don't tend to his every need, he feels neglected and abandoned. Doing what I love doing threatens him—it's as simple as that. He wants a stay-at-home wife—a mother to take care of not only the children but him, too. We've talked this to death. He blames me that I've changed the rules, and in some way, he's right. He thought I'd be happy at home with the kids, but now I'm a psychologist, and I love it; my work fascinates me. I'm not even working that much, but he's always angry and feeling neglected. I want and need to work, and he can't handle it."

In my most brusque and authoritative voice, I imitated him: "Judith, where are the clean towels?" "Judith, don't tell me we're out of toilet paper!" "We're out of milk—again?"

"He complains about me endlessly," I went on, "and it's infuriating. I can't live with his old-fashioned ideas and his inflexibility anymore. He wants a wife whose main role in life is catering to him. I've outgrown him. We've tried therapy and gotten nowhere. We're incompatible. It's over, Ma."

My mother seemed unruffled. She looked almost bored. "This is not new news," she said. "I've heard all this before."

"What's new is, I've had it," I continued. "It's over. I'm getting divorced, Ma. I have an appointment with an attorney next week."

My mother greeted my announcement with a shake of her head. "Nonsense," she said. "Don't do that, Judy. Rachel is eight and Zach is twelve. You're in for some tough years when they're teenagers. And boys need their fathers. Divorce is hard on kids and will be hard on you, too."

"*This* is a hard life," I said. "To live with someone I'm so incompatible with is worse than hard. It's impossible for me. I'm young, Ma, and I have a lifetime. I want more. I want better." I felt like screaming at her, but I kept my voice level. "It's over."

"Do you have someone else?" she asked.

"Ma!" *I can't believe this! Who does she think I am—her?*

My mother's brown eyes flashed. "So what if you're incompatible about some things? Big deal! You have two children, dear, and they're young. And your husband loves those children—I know that." She shrugged. "Don't do it to the kids. All marriages get boring, dear. Men are difficult, and marriage, too. I should know, right?"

Recently widowed for the third time, she spoke from a place of experience. Even if she had never been divorced, she had been alone, and I knew she believed that being married was far better than being alone, even when marriage is difficult, which it always is.

"There's nothing wrong with your husband, dear. Or your marriage. Marriage is not fifty-fifty. I've told you that before. This fifty-fifty thing is just a newfangled trend. When it comes to the home and the kids, women do it all—that's the reality. And Arnie *is* a loving father and a very good provider, let me remind you. You have a good life. You have an easy life, with everything you need. I know you—you don't really like being alone. I remember you after Michael died. Let me be blunt—it didn't take you long to take up with your next-door neighbor. What was his name?"

I felt my stomach tense. Did she have to cavalierly mention the untimely death of Michael, my fiancé who was killed in a freak car accident when I was twenty-three? Yes, I did fall apart and take refuge in the arms of my next-door neighbor, Tom, but what did that have to do with now?

It was as if she were a mind reader. "I hate bringing up Michael and what was his name . . . Oh, yes—Tom! After Michael died, Tom was at your side, day and night, and that's my point. I know you, and you are not good at being alone. If you and Arnie split, you'll probably be quick to find someone new, of course, with his own problems—which might be worse than the ones you have with Arnie. And whoever you find won't be your children's father—and certainly won't love them the way Arnie does. Whoever you find may come with his own kids and an ex-wife to deal with. Then again, you might never find anyone." My mother rolled her eyes again. "If you want to know what I think, don't get divorced. Have an affair. Affairs are harmless. It might cheer you up. It might even hold your marriage together."

I had no idea what I'd expected, but certainly not this piece of advice. I had no idea what to say.

"That's not what I want, Ma." Once again, I had to face the fact that my mother had opened up another wound: how different we were. I looked at my watch. "Gotta go, Ma. My car is at a meter, and I'm running out of time."

Standing at the door, she gave me a peck on the cheek. "You might not like what I have to say, dear, but I'm only telling you what I really think. You wouldn't want me to be phony and just agree with you, would you? I know your marriage is not all you might want, but divorce? It won't be a picnic."

I had no answer for that. Now, years later, I realize what I needed was for her to listen to me—listen carefully, and help me slow down and consider my options carefully. But deep listening was not her strong suit; she was a woman who had been raised pre–women's lib, when women's options were sparse and staying married was generally considered more desirable than risking the alternative.

"Call me when you get home, dear. And think about what I'm saying before you do anything rash. I know I'm repeating myself, but I can't help telling you what I think. Divorce will be hard—on you and on the kids."

Standing at the elevator, sweating, I was more determined than ever to get divorced.

Minutes later, I was stuck in bumper-to-bumper traffic in my car, crossing the East River on the way back to Long Island. I was in a time warp, stuck in the whiteout on the corner of Ninety-Sixth Street and Broadway. Large, wet snowflakes glistened as they drifted down past the red streetlight. The light changed, and my mother and I stepped off the curb, slick with melting snow.

"*I have someone. I have someone. I have someone. I have someone.*" I was stuck in a moment in time that had seared me. How had I forgotten my mother's worldview? What had I expected from her?

Moving Day

Not long after, on a bright, sunny September day in 1983, Arnie officially moved out of the home we had created and lived in together for fifteen years. He was moving into a house he had rented only a few blocks away, but in reality he was moving into another universe. So was I. We both had only a limited awareness of the chaos that lay ahead.

The children had just left for school and I was sitting alone on the nubby tweed couch in my living room when a loud screech of wheels on pavement announced the arrival of the large brown moving van. I had expected it, but I was startled. My hands were clammy and my stomach in knots as I parted the living room drapes a crack and stood, half hidden, peering into the street, watching the van lurch to a halt in front of my house.

Next, Arnie pulled up in his black Oldsmobile Tornado, snug behind the van. He sat, chain smoking, giving orders to the chief honcho of the movers, who stood by his open car window, talking. The mover was wearing a cutoff T-shirt and shorts, and I remember thinking about my hands. The day was mild, but my hands were icy.

Perched on my living room sofa, I sat, watching the movers walk in and out through the front door. They entered empty-handed and left laden with boxes. Hypnotically, I watched Arnie, sitting in his car, scowling and smoking, as the men marched in and out, in and out. First out was the furniture, then the clothing wardrobes, then the boxes—books and records and tapes, boxes of mementos. He took the pastel watercolor of the Golden Gate Bridge that we had bought as an anniversary present on a trip out West; I kept the oil of Yosemite. College notebooks and his trumpet. Fifteen years of dreams and memories, packed up and gone.

Finally, the front door closed for good. Gone. The furniture, the boxes, the moving men, Arnie. Gone. I remember feeling as if I was on a merry-go-round of racing emotions, swinging from numb to hurt to sad to hopeful, uncomfortable with the wild swing, with the uncontrollable emotions racing and raging through my body. After the van left and his black car pulled away, I sat on the living room couch for a long, long time, surprised at how exhausted I was, considering it was not even noon. What surprised me next was the blankness, like the white spaces on the living room walls where pictures once hung. I wondered if I would always feel so empty.

I eventually put on my sneakers and walked down to the ocean. Maybe I would take a run—and find time to drift, dream, and think. The water's edge was dotted with small children and seagulls, the air filled with the mingle of bird calls and children's voices and the pounding of the surf. All I could hear was my insides, mewing.

No jogging today, Jude, I said to myself. *Too tired.*

I wondered if I would ever run again.

The Little Engine
That Could

Not only did I run again, but less than a year later, I ran a ten-mile race, exactly three and a half miles farther than I'd ever run before. Even though my braids had been cut off for more than three decades, when I began that last mile, I felt them slapping against my sweaty back, jogging my memory. I recalled being small, hearing my mother's voice as she read to me from *The Little Engine That Could*, a book I later read to my own children. The clatter of the little blue engine's wheels kept me company on that final stretch, and as I chugged along I heard my mother's singsong voice describing the mountain to me in the very same words I'd read to my own children—*". . . so big, so very, very big!"* When I got to the last tenth of the last mile, when the crowds were cheering and the finish line was visible, my mother's words rang loudly in my ears: *"I think I can! I think I can! I think I can!"* Crossing the finish line in 103 minutes and 13 seconds, as the theme song from *Chariots of Fire* blasted from the speaker, I felt like weeping.

It was when the race was over, and I was milling around, drinking ice-cold soda and sucking on watermelon, that I met

Jonah, tall with deep-set hazel eyes almost hidden behind his long, curly blond hair.

His wife had died only five weeks earlier. Cancer. First in the breast, then, eventually, everywhere. A long, losing fight, which had absorbed and tortured him for three years.

"The funeral was five weeks ago today," he said, as we sat in the grass, cooling our dripping bodies. He wondered if I remembered the torrential rain that Sunday, the day of his wife's funeral.

I remembered the day and the teeming rain well—it was the day I'd taken my daughter dress shopping for Zach's bar mitzvah, only a month off. As Rachel and I darted in and out of stores, dodging the raindrops, I tried to imagine how I'd get through Zach's big day. It would be difficult to be divorced at a time when being a family was so important.

Later, Jonah drove me home. Sitting in his car that muggy May afternoon, sweaty and fatigued and basking in the afterglow of the race, we talked and talked—about what it meant to be alone, about what it was like to mourn a whole way of life that had suddenly evaporated for each of us, for different reasons.

That night, he called. I wasn't really surprised. I had felt that special shudder of excitement as we'd sat in his car, and I figured he had, too.

"Come over after the kids are asleep," I said. I told him I'd call him when the coast was clear. Naturally, that was the night my children found endless excuses to delay bedtime. It was close to eleven when I found myself, wearing freshly applied makeup, answering the doorbell.

Hope Is the Thing
with Feathers

"As the only parent of three kids, I can't stay too long," Jonah whispered, careful not to awaken my sleeping children. That line became our first inside joke, as each night we snuck whatever time we could find to talk or cuddle, massaging each other's wounded, bruised souls.

That year I spent Father's Day, a broiling-hot Sunday afternoon in June, with Jonah and his three children: Ben, fourteen; Matt, eleven; and Samantha, six. As we sat at the outdoor restaurant on a huge, crowded deck overlooking Reynolds Channel, shaded by a green striped awning flapping in the breeze, I remember trying desperately to blot out the other tables, all filled with what seemed to be happy, intact families. *What am I doing here?* I wondered, choking back tears, my heart aching for my own children, who were spending the day with their father, sailing on the boat that had once belonged to us.

Jonah was deeply touched by the gift I gave him for Father's Day. It was one of my favorites, a book of Emily Dickinson's poetry. Nightly, he closed our phone conversations by reading me one of her poems. I still remember his favorite, a poem called "Hope," which inspired his first gift to me, a pink T-shirt with a fragile white feather silk-screened across the back.

Hope is the thing with feathers
That perches in the soul,
And sings the tune without the words
And never stops at all.

For six weeks, we devoured each other. We ran together, biked together, read together, walked the beach, collected feathers, and breathlessly waited for each other's calls and kisses.

Then my consuming appetite for Jonah ended abruptly. I can't say exactly why. It might have been because I met Jerry, or Richard, although at this point I'm not certain about who really did follow Jonah in what felt like an endless string of men. It might have been simply because he became too enamored of me or because he came too close.

The day I ended it still stands out. We had met at the boardwalk to go bike riding. He gave me another T-shirt he had made for me, whose personalized message colorfully and proudly proclaimed I'M A JUDY JUNKY. That gift changed everything.

Telling him was hard.

It really wasn't him, personally, I stammered, trying to explain what I really didn't understand myself: about why I kept drifting from one man to another, experiencing each in his initial newness as fascinating and meaningful, until I lost interest, and how predictably fleeting these experiences were becoming. Recently, I'd noticed that with each new man, the meaningful period was briefer and shorter than with his predecessor. Thinking about the series of passionate lovers who preceded Jonah left me feeling mildly queasy, wondering if it would always be like this.

Solemnly, Jonah listened to me.

"We are really good together," he said, finally.

I nodded—it was true. But my heart was not in it anymore, and I didn't know why. And I didn't have much to say.

Another loss for each of us, picking and tugging at wounds, scars still raw.

The Unexpected Gift of a Freudian Slip

An alarm had gone off in my mind when Ella enthusiastically announced her divorce decision. I was uncomfortable sitting back, "just listening," and perhaps endorsing what appeared to be an impulsive decision. I wanted to stress the importance of her taking time for reflection.

If Ella were to follow through and divorce her husband, Al, the upcoming year would be a crucial time to shore up her resources. Ella was a woman who had never worked outside the home and had no experience earning money or handling the financial realities at the foundation of her upscale, privileged life. Although she was quite pretty, her self-perception as "fat" overrode everything. For the most part, she felt ashamed of her body and her appearance. Married to her high school boyfriend, she also had had no experience with the stresses of dating. Al, a tough, macho bully, was likely to be impossible during the divorce and then, later, perhaps an even worse an ex-husband than he had been a husband. Ella came from a conservative family and social world where she was likely to be stigmatized and blamed for a failed marriage. While her marriage was far from perfect, before she ended it, she needed to develop new tools to deal with life on the other side of divorce. Goodness knows, I'd entered into a divorce without much of a solid plan.

My Freudian slip had taken us into unexpected territory. Warning her that her decision might be a "mistake" had, on the one hand, put me in the role of a critic, rather than of a support. However, it also inspired me to push her—and myself, too—into the reflective mode that imagery inspires. Once again, I found myself examining my own divorce—and my mother. At a time when I might have benefited from being helped to think carefully about the consequences of divorce, her response had frustrated me and alienated me from her. It might even have incited me into rebelling against her. One thing was certain. What I'd needed was a thoughtful conversation, rather than my mother's simplistic advice: "Don't get divorced; have an affair."

Nonetheless, I had to face it—my first reaction to Ella was an unconscious blunder. I'd told her divorce was a mistake. I'd echoed my mother!

As my mind swung between my mother's reaction to me and my reaction to Ella, something inside me shifted. It dawned on me that maybe, just as I'd wanted to protect and warn Ella, my mother had done her best to try to shield me from what she called "leaping from the frying pan" of a difficult marriage "into the fire" of divorce. Like Ella, my mother was a woman without a career or financial resources. She had lived in an era when divorce was stigmatized. Perhaps she had been more thoughtful than I'd realized; perhaps, faced with a difficult marriage, she'd chosen wisely for herself.

Notwithstanding my fulfilling and rich work life, my own divorce journey had been far more harrowing than I'd ever imagined. Single parenting, joint custody, financial stresses, and a decade of floundering relationships had taken their toll on not only me but also my children. My divorce had been more devastating than I could ever have anticipated. I had been unprepared for all I was forced to face. Although I had survived, and perhaps thrived, the wounds of my divorce had left scars on my now grown children, as well as on my own life in ways I never could have anticipated.

"One last thing," Ella continued. "Last week, when I got home from our appointment, I threw away the spare ribs. I kept asking myself the question you ask me over and over: *What are you really hungry for?* I'm not sure I know the answer, but it's certainly not cold spare ribs!"

PART FIVE:

Mother-Daughter Complications

Think about a story you have told repeatedly about your mother, whether it is about something humorous, tragic, or difficult, or a moment of happiness between you. Imagine telling it again, to someone who is listening attentively. Notice how you feel in your body as you tell this story. What does this story tell you about the mother who raised you? Why do you like to tell it?

Leaving Home

According to Joseph Campbell, the author of *The Power of Myth* and whose life work was dedicated to studying the mythology of numerous cultures, we must be willing to take risks and leave the familiar to grow. Every adventure out in the world will test us in unexpected ways, bringing us in touch with our strengths and resources, as well as our shortcomings and vulnerabilities. Leaving home is the first step.

Therapy is also a mythic journey away from home. By facing the places in ourselves where we are stuck and by being honest with ourselves, we become freer, more expansive human beings.

As a therapist, I have been deeply moved, often changed, by the work my patients do. Witnessing the complications of so many mother-daughter relationships has given me a wider perspective on my own struggles. Ultimately, I have come to see my own story from a mythic perspective, as part of a universal story. Like Campbell's travelers, I have come to appreciate my own wounds and strengths, and my mother's as well.

In this section, I will share how four encounters offered me the opportunity to grow as I reexamined my relationship with my mother.

Marcy, Daughter of Elizabeth: Pain Is Never the Last Step

M arcy, a twenty-one-year-old senior at Adelphi University, arrived in my office, tormented by her latest failed diet, the Scarsdale. Broad-shouldered, with long, curly blond hair, she had struggled with yo-yo dieting for more than a decade. Now, well over two hundred pounds at five foot seven, she was determined to lose fifty pounds. Could I help her lose weight?

We began therapy, retracing her history of binge eating, shame, and restrictive dieting that inevitably followed, a cycle that began in her childhood. We spent many sessions uncovering forgotten chapters of frustration and sadness, where she reconnected with the pain of being her mother's disappointing, overweight daughter, dragged from one diet doctor to another.

The first step of therapy is always creating a safe, trusting relationship, the bedrock of healing. I tried to listen carefully to Marcy in a way that validated her pain and acknowledged that some things can never be fixed and some grief never goes away. It didn't take long for Marcy's rage, buried beneath her shame, to emerge, first at herself, eventually at her mother.

While in the short run, blowing up and discharging anger offer a momentary thrill, angry discharges rarely lead to healing and instead intensify disconnections and often remorse. But holding anger in is not the answer; doing so not only raises our blood pressure, leaving us at risk for strokes and heart problems, but does not get at what always lies beneath the anger: pain. Often I have shared my grandmother's adage, which I try to access when I feel triggered: "Blowing up with anger generally poisons only your own system and rarely changes anything."

Marcy had been working with me in therapy for six months when I began worrying she might get stuck in a cycle of mother blaming. At that point, I suggested inviting her mother to join us for a session.

It was our first family meeting. Tossing her long blond hair back from her scowling face, Marcy glared at Elizabeth, her mother, and spoke through clenched teeth. "You know I came here to lose weight, right, Mom?" she began.

Her mother nodded.

"I've learned a lot here in therapy, Mom, and I want to tell you: I know you thought you were being helpful to me, Mom, buying me all that special 'diet' food when I was a kid, but there's something I never understood before."

Marcy's delivery struck me. Each time she pronounced the word "Mom," she raised her voice and narrowed her eyes. She sounded more and more like a machine gun. She stared straight into her mother's eyes. "Your 'helpfulness' was where my weight problem began. My food problem began with you, Mom."

Elizabeth broke eye contact with her daughter and stared at the floor.

"Don't look away. I need you to listen to what I'm telling you, Mom. You must have known that dragging me from diet doctor to diet doctor was a waste of time. It didn't help, did it? Putting me on those diet pills—didn't you know they would screw up my metabolism?" she asked.

Marcy raced on, oblivious to the fact that tears were gathering in the corners of Elizabeth's eyes. Marcy's face was tight; her voice strident and loud.

"I want to let you know what I've learned," Marcy continued. "Dieting screwed up my body and my mind. Instead of tapping into my body and learning to recognize whether I was hungry or full, I listened to these crazy doctors and their rigid ideas. Basically, I was starving—and what do you think starving people do, Mom? They eat! So I started eating, and eating turned into bingeing. I got fatter and fatter, Mom. But you continued with those diet doctors and the pills. Can you imagine what it was like for nine-year-old me to have to make excuses to my friends when you picked me up at school to take me to the fat doctor?"

As I listened to Marcy, I watched her mother slump further back into the couch. I felt torn. One part of me connected with the enraged daughter who had stuffed down her feelings of fury and shame for too long. Another part of me was worried about Elizabeth, who I assumed was unprepared for her daughter's wrath. I had known Marcy planned to confront her mother, but the anger she communicated in her tone of voice and her facial expressions stunned me. I was taken aback to hear my words—albeit distorted—coming out of Marcy's mouth in a vicious manner.

Earlier in therapy, I had explained to Marcy that in the past decade we had learned a lot about a new theory of weight and body size, a genetically determined body-fat set point, which dictates a ten-to-twenty-pound weight range. Set point theory helps us understand why dieting, exercise, and diet pills are not a permanent source of weight loss, because basically our bodies resist attempts to change that set point weight. When our weight dips below our genetically determined range, our brain sends our body a signal to adjust our appetite and metabolism, increasing hunger and cravings and reducing metabolism and satiety. I had hypothesized that perhaps Elizabeth was unaware of this new information but had been trying to be helpful in encouraging her daughter to lose weight. Sometimes, I'd said, when parents try to be "helpful," they make unwitting mistakes. But now, sitting with Marcy and Elizabeth, I felt anxious. My intent had been to raise Marcy's understanding of and compassion for herself, but I realized I'd fueled a brutal attack.

"Marcy, perhaps you can speak a bit more softly—maybe turn down the volume a bit?" I suggested gently, as Elizabeth squirmed. "I know this is hard for you to hear, Elizabeth, but it's important that Marcy knows you're listening and taking in her pain."

Marcy took a deep breath, and when she spoke, her voice was soft. "I've just spent months dealing with my childhood misery. It seemed all you cared about was what I weighed. You had no interest in understanding how I felt."

"That's not true, honey," Elizabeth said, eyes downcast.

I cringed again. I knew from raising my own children that sometimes what I did in their best interest could seem uncaring, even punitive to them. I remember how devastated my nine-year-old daughter, Rachel, had been when I'd refused to let her friend sleep over. She'd been unable to hear my concern about her friend's severe cough, and even later, when it turned out the friend had indeed come down with a wicked flu, Rachel remained sulky, unforgiving of me.

While I knew that Marcy needed to express her pain, I wanted to support Elizabeth as well.

"I think your mom needs a moment," I said to Marcy. "Let's give her a chance to respond."

After a long pause, Elizabeth finally spoke up in a low voice. "I have to apologize. I admit that I did drag you to one diet doctor after another, but I want to tell you some things you may not know or may not have thought about." She paused. "You know that I was an overweight kid, right?"

"You've mentioned it," Marcy said, with a chilly edge to her voice.

"I don't think I ever shared all the details of my own miserable childhood," her mother said tearfully. "I know you know I was always overweight, but there was more. As a kid, I was the fat daughter at home and the fattest girl in my class. I didn't want you to go through what I went through. I was teased and humiliated—at home and at school. I never wanted you to feel that way; that's why I wanted to help you lose weight!"

Marcy's eyes were wide.

"Did you know that your mother was teased about being the fattest girl in the class?" I asked, wanting Marcy to absorb her mother's pain and humiliation.

Marcy shook her head no. "I knew you were overweight, but you never told me anything about being teased," she said to her mother.

I turned to Elizabeth. "Can you tell her more? Can you tell her what that was like for you?"

Elizabeth sighed. "I was really fat. Very fat. You know my sisters, Aunt Joan and Aunt Bonnie? I was the oldest of the three daughters, all toothpick thin but me. My parents were athletic, and so were my sisters. I knew I was a disappointment to my parents; I was clumsy, chubby, and unathletic. And school was a nightmare—I was always the last to be picked in gym, always. I was so ashamed." By now Elizabeth's voice had dropped so low I could barely hear her.

"Your voice is fading away; this seems so painful for you to talk about," I said. Elizabeth nodded. "So thank you for being so open. It's important for Marcy to understand where you were coming from."

"From the time I was very young, I was overweight," Elizabeth continued, seeming to perk up. "I don't really know why—maybe it was my genes. My mother told me I took after her mother, Grandma Suzanna, who died before I was born. At home they called me 'chubby.' Eventually that's what I was called at school, too. How I hate that word!" By now, Elizabeth's voice was wobbling again.

"Tell Marcy what that was like for you, being called 'chubby.'"

"I hated school, and I especially hated my teachers for not stopping those mean kids. Most of all, I hated myself for being fat. That's why I felt so distressed when I saw you gaining weight. I felt I had to do everything in my power to help you lose weight. I'm so sorry that I embarrassed you. I want you to understand one thing: I did what I did to spare you my fate. I only wanted to spare you pain. I really did the best I could do."

Her words echoed—"I only wanted to spare you pain. I did the best I could do"—and my mother's face appeared, saying, "I did the best I could do. I tried to do my best."

"Tell your mom what you're hearing her say," I told Marcy, coaching her in the active-listening technique I'd found so valuable. I wanted her to mirror not only her mother's words but also her emotions.

"You did the best you could do. You wanted to spare me pain," she said softly.

"What are you feeling as you mirror your mother's words?" I asked, wanting to check in on Marcy's emotional state. Often people will echo what they think they are supposed to say, without really taking in the emotional message.

"I feel for you, Ma," Marcy said quietly.

For the rest of the session, as I went back and forth, helping mother and daughter speak slowly and listen carefully to one another, something softened in each of them. As Marcy took in her mother's painful childhood—and her mother's intention to protect her—I hoped she was able to create a new narrative and see herself as loved and lovable, rather than as neglected and ignored by a careless, self-absorbed mother. In coaching Elizabeth to listen carefully to her daughter's pain, I was hopeful she might integrate a new way of being an empathic mother.

"We are going to stop in a moment," I said. "I'd like to check in with you both. How do you feel now compared with how you felt when we sat down together an hour ago?" My intention was to help them realize that expressing anger and sharing painful feelings is always scary and risky but can actually lead to healing.

Marcy moved closer to Elizabeth on the couch and put her hand on her mother's. Neither said a word for a long moment. I was surprised when Elizabeth spoke up.

"I think this session has helped me. I'm learning new things here about how to talk to my daughter. Maybe I can come in another time?"

Marcy nodded, but I hesitated. I wanted to have a chance to meet with and check in with Marcy alone, before meeting with her mother again. We set up two separate appointments, the first confirming my regular session with Marcy and then scheduling a different appointment for the three of us. When mother and daughter walked out the door, I felt a sense of hope. Perhaps we were laying the groundwork for a new kind of communication and relatedness for the two of them.

That night, driving home from my office, I found myself mulling over my work with Marcy and Elizabeth. Elizabeth's words had jarred me during the session, and now they jumped back out at me again. "I did drag you to diet doctors, but I was just following doctor's orders." I had seen on her face what I believed was genuine regret when she explained to Marcy, "I only tried to do my best." As I replayed this scene and the words "following doctor's orders" echoed, I felt myself begin to break out in a cold sweat. And I knew why.

I'd mercilessly berated my mother for "following doctor's orders" when she'd tried to explain the way she deceived me about my tonsillectomy—but now, listening to these words in this new context, I was pushed to reexamine my own reaction. Perhaps my mother's "crime" for deceiving me with a "birthday party" wasn't as out of the box as I might have thought. Like Elizabeth, my mother had followed doctor's orders, instead of preparing eight-year-old me to face a hospitalization and surgery. It didn't take long before it occurred to me that I was able to tap into my compassion to help Marcy offer forgiveness to her mother while I was still chastising my own mother for the same excuse.

As a therapist, I had compassion for both Marcy's suffering and Elizabeth's, but as a daughter, I still sat in judgment of my own mother, as I had for decades. Why, I had to ask myself, was it so hard for me to find compassion for my own mother? I took a deep breath, as I realized this was something I needed to "bookmark," a phrase I used with my patients when it was clear we had not gotten to the bottom of a piece of unfinished business.

By now I was at home, sitting in my driveway, but the two phrases from the session gnawed at me: "following doctor's orders" and "I only tried to do my best." The phrases echoed, at first evoking my painful tonsillectomy experience. I said the words again, slowly, to myself. To my surprise, other thoughts came up. There had been times when I'd been certain I was "doing my best"—getting divorced was one example—only to realize later on that I had gravely underestimated how divorce would impact my children.

Suddenly, my father's face appeared, and I was pulled into another level of pain.

It was Christmas Eve 1971, my father's fifty-fourth birthday, and our family was gathered for a celebratory dinner at my childhood home, where my parents still lived. The results of the bladder cancer surgery, initially deemed a success, had been overturned. The cancer had spread, and now, unbeknownst to him, he was living with a terminal diagnosis. Although we knew death was inevitable, we had no way of knowing we were almost out of time. In reality, he had less than three weeks to live.

It was cold and windy that December morning when I bundled up four-month-old Zach and we made our way from my Upper West Side apartment down to the Long Island Railroad station. Ever since my father's terminal diagnosis, three months earlier, I'd been filled with gloom and despair, but today I had a mission. I'd help my mom organize my dad's birthday dinner, and I'd get to spend some time with my father. I hoped my sunny baby, who had just learned to smile, would cheer them up before my husband and brother arrived for dinner that night.

I'd been out at my parents' home for what had been already a long day; by now, the sky was dark, even though it was just past five. Zach had woken from his afternoon nap cooing and smiling; I had just taken him from his crib and come downstairs. I was about to enter the kitchen, when, passing through the hallway, I stopped, seeing my father sitting in his favorite blue velvet chair by the hi-fi, listening to *La Traviata*, reading the libretto.

His brown crewneck sweater and khaki pants hung on his frail body. Standing in the doorway, with Zach snuggled on my shoulder, I was unable to move. I was struck by how weak my father had become in these past few months. In August, we had been playing tennis; by October, we'd learned his cancer had spread. The questions had plagued me ever since his terminal diagnosis rose up. How will my mother cope when he is gone? How will she cope without him, having been married since eighteen? How will we all be without him? And what is this like for him, to be withering away at fifty-three? It's a moment I will never forget: standing in the living room doorway, wishing I could reach out yet not knowing what to say.

Only moments later, I was in the kitchen, slicing tomatoes and peeling carrots for a salad. A cooing Zach was perched in his baby seat beside me on the counter while my mother orchestrated the preparation of my dad's favorite birthday meal: brisket, roasted new potatoes, noodle pudding, steamed vegetables, salad, and her delicious chocolate mousse cake. Ordinarily, my father, a fastidious, weight-conscious eater who had maniacally pursued healthy eating before it was in vogue, would have balked at two starches, but he'd been concerned because his weight was slipping. Over and over, he'd said, "How is it possible I'm losing weight, with all the starches and sweets my wife is feeding me?" By now, I had become a master at keeping peace and simply dodged his questions and the conversation. Sometimes I'd leave the room to avoid his piercing blue eyes—I was certain he'd be suspicious if he looked at me closely.

Suddenly, an unusually tender *Traviata* aria filled the room at top volume. For the music to blast into the kitchen, separated from the living room by two solid doors, there had to be something wrong with the hi-fi system—or my father.

"Watch Zach, Ma," I exclaimed, as I rushed into the living room, where I froze, looking at my pasty-faced father, hooked up to his oxygen tank. Eyes wide open, he was gazing at the ceiling. His mouth was open, too. The eerie expression on his thin face terrified me. Was he okay? Had he passed out? Could he have had a stroke? Could he be dead?

"Daddy, Daddy!" I wailed, rushing over to him.

Startled, he focused his eyes on mine and pushed the off button on the hi-fi.

"I blasted this damn thing because I have no voice," he said gruffly. "No one can hear me! I'm losing my voice, and you can't hear me in the kitchen with the doors closed and all that damn chatter going on." His breathing was labored, his voice low. "On top of everything else that's falling apart in this body of mine, no one can hear me unless I scream, and I can't scream or yell anymore, because I don't have the air. My voice is gone! If I need anyone or anything, this is the only way I can get it."

He reached over and grabbed the hi-fi knob, and within a moment, as if to show his prowess, a booming operatic melody filled the air again. A moment later, he lowered the hi-fi, and his voice, when he next spoke contained an odd combination of exhaustion, bitterness, anger, and fear. "You people are telling me I'm getting better, but I'm not getting better, am I?"

Thankfully, he didn't pause for a response. What would I have said?

"I am not better. I don't feel a damn bit better. I feel worse." After a pause, he added, "Much worse," and then gazed at the floor.

I have no idea how I calmed my father down. Probably I apologized for the kitchen door being closed. Probably I asked him what he wanted—a glass of water? Something to eat? A scotch? He wasn't supposed to drink, but I knew it was far too late for alcohol to do much harm, and perhaps, I thought, a sip of Dewar's Red Label, his favorite scotch, would pep him up. Or maybe he just needed assistance fixing the regulator on his oxygen tank.

I don't remember what I said, but what remains with me today is my horror at the realization that my father was facing death alone because his oncologist had advised my mother, my brother, and me to keep his terminal condition from him. My father must have intuitively known the truth, but we held on to our secret and kept to our "you are recovering" story, to the very end. Later, when he was gone, my brother and I would ponder our rationale. Why had we chosen to follow "doctor's orders"—and at what cost? Had my father faced death alone because we had not been brave enough to challenge the doctor? Because we were too nervous about speaking about death—a taboo subject?

In retrospect, I know that if my brother and I had stood up to my mother, had we taken a stand, we might have created a different ending for my dad. We might have been able to tell him what he meant to each of us. Perhaps we would have wept together. Wouldn't it have been better if we had all been able to cry together, rather than privately? Wouldn't my father have loved to hear me tell him that for the rest of my life, when I skied in the bitter cold or when I hit a winning tennis lob, I'd think of him?

Now, I know I must forgive myself. It was 1971, and talking about death with the dying was not mainstream. Disregarding doctor's orders wasn't usual.

As I sat in the driveway, my eyes were full. To recognize that I was guilty of the very "crime" I had accused my mother of was mind-numbing. I felt sick, horrified to admit that what I did to my father when he was dying was what my mother had done to me when I was scheduled for a tonsillectomy—I kept a secret; I followed orders. It was only later that I would forgive myself as I learned to accept the harsh reality that it is human nature to repeat the past. I had grown up in a world where keeping secrets was not only condoned but acceptable and practiced routinely. Over time, I would come to accept that all of us can slip into unconscious reenactments. The intergenerational transmission of trauma spares no one.

Debra, Daughter of Sandra:
When a Wounded Daughter
Becomes a Wounded Mother

Sandra's bracelets jangled as she came into my office and sat down on the couch next to her daughter, Debra. She was a tall woman in her early forties, wearing a tailored pantsuit. She immediately began to gush, "We have good news!"

This surprised me. Most people coming in for an initial consultation start with the bad news. What could this kind of introduction mean?

There certainly was good news. Debra had been accepted, early action, to Radcliffe. The bad news was that ever since her acceptance, a month earlier, she had been losing weight, which was what had motivated Sandra's call.

Sandra's bracelets continued to rattle as she spoke animatedly. She described her daughter as a fussy baby, a picky eater, who was now never hungry and avoided all carbs and sugar. Sandra now suspected Debra was water loading, filling up on water to stave off hunger.

First impression: Sandra seemed bright, articulate, and concerned, and usually a concerned parent is a welcome relief, but I noticed immediately how put off I felt. Her jarring, non-stop narrative and her jangling bracelets seemed to take up all the space in the room.

Slender, dark-haired Debra sat in silence, eyes on the floor.

When Sandra finished speaking, I asked her to step into the waiting room so that Debra and I could talk privately. Clearly, I needed to set some boundaries with this overbearing mother.

When the door shut, Debra looked me straight in the eye. "Thank you," she said, nodding her head toward the door. "My mom is so bossy—she acts like I can't take care of myself." Debra's jaw tightened as she told me this.

Debra described the fight she'd had with her mother that morning, when Sandra insisted Debra wear rubber boots to school because it was raining. Debra tried to explain that she did not want to spend the day trudging around school with sweaty feet, but Sandra ignored her explanations.

"I wound up wearing these damn boots all day in school," Debra said, with tears in her eyes. She stared off for a while into the middle distance. "She's so busy telling me what to do all the time, and she's never willing to listen to anything I say."

She went on to describe other boundary violations: the dress Debra wore to her sweet-sixteen party was the one she chose from the several Sandra had brought home. And when Debra had been in camp, her mother had redecorated her room.

"She's already written to college and gotten me application forms to apply to be editor of the school newspaper. And when it comes to my eating, she's a nonstop hawk. She doesn't understand that I've really just lost my appetite and I don't want to lose weight. She dragged me to my pediatrician, who said my weight is normal—and I haven't lost my period. And now she's dragged me here to see you. I'm fine—she's the one who needs therapy, not me."

The traditional understanding of anorexia nervosa is that it is a disorder of control. What one eats is one of the few domains a teenager can control. It was clear to me that Sandra was a take-over parent, but I wondered, did Debra need to develop a life-threatening eating disorder to get some space from her mother and to control her own life?

I invited Sandra back into the office and encouraged Debra to talk about what was on her mind. To my surprise, Debra spoke up, timidly at first, and to my surprise again, Sandra admitted she could be controlling, but, she explained, her reasons were well founded.

"My daughter is so shy, and I'm afraid she won't take advantage of all that college can offer. She's an exceptionally talented writer, but . . ." Sandra turned to Debra and said, "It would be a shame if you didn't apply to be editor; Deb, you are such a good writer!"

While Sandra was doing something affirmative, confirming Debra's strengths, I wasn't sure she was truly aware of her impact.

"Sandra, I see how much you care about your daughter and how much you care about being a good parent, but I want you to pause for a minute." I stopped talking, and both Sandra and Debra looked at me. I lowered my voice. "Take a look at Debra," I said to Sandra. "How do you think she's responding to you?"

Sadness swept across Sandra's face. "She isn't listening. She probably thinks I'm too much." She sounded despondent.

"Can you ask her how she feels?"

"She looks upset."

I felt impatient as, once again, Sandra answered for her daughter. "Sandra, would it be okay if I coached you?"

Sandra nodded.

"Rather than telling me how you think Debra feels, can you *ask* her?"

Sandra turned to her daughter, immediately cooperative. "How do you feel, honey?"

Debra looked her mother straight in the eyes. "Mom, you are too much! Get a life!"

Sandra looked shattered. "What do you mean? I have a life!" Sandra turned to me. "I have a life, and I work overtime. Between my full-time job teaching and everything else I do for our family . . ."

I paused as Sandra kept talking. How could I help her see the impact of her over-caring behaviors?

"Sandra," I eventually said, "I see how hard you work at being a good mother, but I'm worried you're getting caught up in being too helpful. Can I explain what I mean?" She nodded, and I continued, "A caring parent can easily slide into over-parenting; that can be a problem as destructive as being a negligent parent—which you certainly are not."

Sandra broke eye contact and looked crestfallen.

"I think I said something that bothered you," I said. "Was it when I said that over-parenting could be destructive?"

Sandra shook her head no.

"Sandra, I saw your face drop, and I'm not sure exactly what happened." I took a chance and continued speaking, hoping I wasn't going to sound like I was lecturing her. "Being a good parent is never simple, and it's easy for us, as parents, to get triggered by our own childhoods," I said. "Can we take a moment and go back to your senior year of high school? What was life like for you when you were Debra's age?"

Sandra's face clouded over, and she remained quiet. In the silence that followed, I hoped I hadn't gone further than Sandra was willing to go in looking backward; asking a parent to recall being the age of a troubled child is sometimes fruitful but often risks evoking early pain.

It took Sandra a minute to speak up. She finally said, "When I was Debra's age?" She sighed. "I was on my own."

"Tell me about being on your own," I said.

Sandra's story then poured out.

She had grown up in Brooklyn, daughter of hardworking Polish immigrants who came from a tiny town outside Warsaw. She was ashamed of her mother, who spoke broken English, didn't drive, and wore frumpy clothing. "She always looked sloppy and old-fashioned, never even wearing a bra."

"Never even wearing a bra," I repeated, which opened up a chapter of Sandra's teenage years.

When Sandra was in seventh grade, she wanted a bra. To her braless mother, for whom finances were always a problem, a bra was a "foolish extravagance."

"Thankfully, my best friend Beth's mother invited me to tag along when the two of them went bra shopping." As Sandra moved into her teen years, Ruth, Beth's mom, became a second mother to Sandra. But Sandra's gratitude was mixed with humiliation. Why couldn't her own mother have been the one who took her shopping? One thing was for sure: Sandra vowed she'd never be like or look like her mother. "That's why I work hard today at looking put-together."

"You do a fantastic job," I said, moved by her story and impressed at her insight.

Our mothers are our first teachers. Regardless of whether we imitate them or rebel against them, we internalize their essence, and it shapes us. As conscious adults, we can choose which parts of our parents we want to imitate and which parts we want to discard, but when we're children, our early identifications—positive and negative—are not conscious.

"Being on your own—what was that like?" I asked.

Like her daughter, Sandra had been an excellent high school student. Upon graduation, she'd been accepted to Brooklyn College, and the summer after high school, she and her boyfriend, Randy, went to work at Kutsher's Country Club, in the Catskill Mountains, to earn some money—she as a waitress, he as a busboy. Their plan was to return to Brooklyn after the summer and start college in September.

But at Kutsher's, Sandra met Rick, a handsome trumpet player in the swing band. Rick, ten years older, swept her off her feet. She dropped Randy and was elated when Rick invited her to move in with him.

"Forget college," Rick had advised.

"The rest is history," Sandra said sadly. By the time the summer was over, she was pregnant. Rick wanted to marry her, and when she called home, her father was in Poland and her mother told her, "Do whatever feels right to you."

"I followed my heart and did what I thought was best," Sandra said. "I married Rick—a man I hardly knew."

Within a few months, she realized he was an alcoholic. A year later, Sandra and her baby, little Terry (Debra's older brother), were back in Brooklyn, living with Sandra's parents. Sandra's mother watched the baby while Sandra worked as a salesgirl during the day and took college classes at night. Eventually she met Bill, her second husband, Debra's father.

"Debra, when I was your age, I thought I knew everything, and in fact I knew nothing," Sandra admitted.

I thanked Sandra for sharing her story, before asking what I've found to be a pivotal question: "If your mother was sitting here with us today, what would you like to tell her?"

For a moment, Sandra remained silent and stared at the ground. When she looked up and made eye contact, her eyes were full. "I'd like to tell her, 'Mom, I needed you! Where were you when I needed you so?'"

I asked Sandra to repeat her question to her mother, and each time she said the words, "I needed you! Where were you when I needed you?" her face fell.

I told Sandra how touched I was listening to her story and hearing her acknowledge her own early sense of loss and abandonment. When I spoke, I tried to go slowly, checking in with her. "Now I have an inkling of something I didn't really understand," I told her. "It's as if you made a commitment never to abandon your daughter the way you were abandoned."

Sandra's face dropped again. Had I goofed?

"I think I hit a nerve," I said. "Was it the word 'abandoned'?"

Tears gathered in the corners of Sandra's eyes, but she swept them aside. "That's the word my husband, Bill, uses all the time whenever we talk about my childhood, and it upsets me to hear that word but maybe it's true. He says my parents neglected me. But my mother couldn't help it. I know she loved me, she just didn't know how to be a better parent."

My heart went out to Sandra. I knew I was listening to a wounded daughter who needed to protect her idealized parents. Many people attempt to deny the reality of their own childhood losses. The idea that it is too late to be lovingly parented as they needed to be during childhood can be too painful to bear; thus, they deny that need and transform it into an overprotectiveness or overinvestment in their own children. Sandra had become a helicopter parent because she didn't want Debra to fall through the cracks as she had. On an unconscious level, over-parenting served multiple needs; it not only allowed her to feel she was a better parent than her own parents, but protected her from knowing the depths of her own neglect.

By now, Sandra was crying. "Deb," she said, turning to her daughter, "I so desperately want you to have an easier life than I had! I want you to get everything out of college that I didn't—I couldn't. For me, college was so complicated. Going to school while working and single parenting was hard! But you have a great opportunity." She paused, before saying something that surprised me. "I realize that I can't keep telling you what you need. I should back off and let you lead your own life."

Of course, Sandra's story reminded me of my mother's. Like my mother, Sandra had forfeited college because of an unplanned pregnancy. But their similarities stopped there; the two embraced opposite parenting styles. Sandra was over-involved, hovering over Debra, while my mother seemed emotionally disconnected. If, as I hypothesized, Sandra's kangaroo style compensated for what she didn't get as a child, what had happened to my mom, who had become an ostrich, content to consistently put her head in the sand? This was a question I would return to repeatedly, unable to unlock the puzzle of my mother.

One of the things that impressed me about Sandra was her emotional complexity. She was able to acknowledge her love of, as well as her resentment toward, her own parents. In contrast, my mother had a one-dimensional, "perfect parents" story. Did my mother's idealistic stance defend her from a grief that I was unaware of and that may have kept her frozen, inhibiting her psychological development?

Although my work with Debra and Sandra offered no concrete answers, it aroused my curiosity and led me to new questions about my mother. What might have occurred that left her so fearful of seeing the complexity of her own parents, who may have had many strengths but probably had a few limitations as well? Had her development frozen at eighteen, when, instead of going to Goucher College, she married my father? She must have experienced a lot: grief, shame, disappointment, and humiliation—did these feelings coalesce into a state of denial? What had occurred to trap her in her own web, primitively defensive of her "perfect parents"? These were conversations I'd never had with my mother. The story I'd heard, over and over, was that two lovebirds had eloped, happily.

There is power in naming our losses. Sandra and Debra grew closer when they could talk about what had been hidden and what needed to be said, reminding me that the ability to relive and talk about trauma in the presence of a supportive person allows the healing process to unfold.

Andrea, Daughter of Jeanne:
All You Need Is Love

We had been meeting for several months when Andrea, a twenty-nine-year-old graduate student, arrived at our session "feeling fat." I was pleased when, after several months of therapy, Andrea became aware that feeling fat was a signal that something she could not put into words was bothering her. "Feeling fat" was shorthand for something disturbing she could not yet name.

I asked her to recall when this fat feeling began. She shrugged and looked at me blankly. Was she shrugging off unwanted thoughts? Or was it me she was shrugging off?

"The fat feeling began last night. Dinner was over, and I was sitting at the kitchen table, alone, in the dark, eating rye bread." After a moment of silence, a trickle of tears leaked out, along with her story. As dinner ended, Andrea's live-in boyfriend, Ben, announced he had been fired. Again. They had been together for six years, and he had lost more than a handful of jobs. For yet another month, he would be unable to pay his share of the rent. For several minutes, Andrea described how she had tried to be calm. Finally, she'd thought she would explode, so she expressed her disappointment and frustration. Ben had remained silent.

"You finished?" he had said harshly, before he got up from the table and stormed out of the apartment, leaving Andrea alone, feeling isolated and abandoned.

Sitting in my office, as Andrea continued telling me about the previous evening's trouble, she repeated the phrase, "I'm stuck. I'm stuck."

"'Stuck'—can you say more? Stuck with what?" I asked. She shrugged.

"With Ben? With the rent money? With yourself?" I asked.

She shrugged again. I noticed I felt exhausted, as if the words she was speaking were hollow and I'd been dragged into a deep hole. The energy had drained from our session.

Traumatic experiences are usually wordless. I wondered if her energy was hidden in her body. "Are you willing to do an experiment?" I asked.

She nodded her head, and I asked her to slow down and check in with her body. We did a slow body scan, and I invited her to breathe into any stuck place in her body.

To my surprise, Andrea placed her right hand over her left shoulder blade. "Right here," she said, "This is where I am stuck."

"Be with your stuck place," I said, "Stay with your shoulder blade a moment. Sense it. Hug it. What is it like to be with your shoulder blade?"

"It feels hard, like a lava rock."

"And what's that like, to be with your lava rock?"

"I'm stuck. I can't really move. It weighs me down."

"Can you say that to your lava rock? Tell it that it weighs you down."

"You weigh me down."

"What does the lava rock say?"

"I'm crushing you; I'm pinning you down; you're stuck with me forever."

I continued inviting Andrea to speak to the lava rock, and in a moment I noticed her mouth drooping.

"I wonder if your drooping mouth has something to say to the lava rock," I said.

Her eyes remained closed, before she spoke aloud. "Get off! I want you to get off me. Get off!" She was emphatic, but her voice remained barely a whisper.

"About the wanting: Where in your body is that feeling?" My question was aimed at helping her access both her needs and her energy. Many women have been trained to serve others and have trouble knowing and expressing their own wants and needs. Articulating one's "wants" is a skill that takes practice and a willingness to risk challenging the givens and facing the unknown.

"It's in my heart."

"Can you talk to your heart?"

"Help me, help me," Andrea whispered.

For a moment or two, we went back and forth. I encouraged Andrea to speak up, and each time, her voice got louder and louder.

"I'm speaking more loudly, but the lava rock doesn't budge and it doesn't hear my heart."

"How long have you known the lava rock?" I asked.

"Since high school."

When I asked Andrea to go back to the time when her heavy heart met the lava rock, she began to sob, as she recalled a series of unhappy endings to relationships with high school boyfriends. Sad and lonely, she had turned to food and fallen into a pattern of bingeing and purging.

"When you think back now, what did you need?" I asked Andrea.

"I guess I needed someone to talk to." After a brief pause, she said, "It's so good to talk about this with you."

"Take a moment and let yourself be with that place inside that feels good," I suggested. Savoring our positive experiences builds resilience.

Andrea sat in silence for a long moment, before saying, "And now I'm remembering being with my mother when I was young, home from school, sick."

Wanting to deepen her experience of what it felt like to be vulnerable and get her needs met, I encouraged her to explore that moment. "Go back in time and see yourself with your mom. Take in the scene. What is happening?"

"I must have been about ten years old. I see my mom stroking my hair."

"Take a moment and go back and be with little Andrea and her mother; see her mother stroking her hair."

Andrea began to cry again. "I haven't seen my mom in months," she said, and began reminiscing about how happy she had been to leave home after high school and get away from her parents, especially her tyrannical father, but how now, it was so hard for her to be so far away from her family, across the country.

"Perhaps you can take a minute to be with your mom now," I suggested. "See yourself with her as she strokes your hair. You don't have to say anything if you don't want to. It's okay to sit in the silence."

Andrea continued to cry; then she spontaneously stopped and smiled.

"I feel warm and mushy. Now I'm remembering that my mom gave me a birthday party in our backyard. It was hot, and we had all my friends over to swim in a plastic pool. I must have been four or five years old." To her surprise, one image prompted another. Next, she saw herself sitting on her mother's lap after she'd fallen off her bicycle. "My mom was humming her favorite song by the Beatles, 'All You Need Is Love.' I must have heard that song a hundred times growing up."

"What's it like to stay with that Beatles song and with the image of your mother being there when you fell off your bike?"

Looking over at me, Andrea said, "I see her stroking my hair and scratching my back, like she used to do when I was young."

"Stay with these images," I said. When I asked her how she felt sharing these memories now, with me, Andrea shrugged. "What happens if, instead of shrugging, you look into my eyes?"

Andrea looked directly at me and smiled. "I feel good— warm and mushy."

"Know that this feeling, the one you have inside of you, is yours. It's something you can come back to whenever you want."

When Andrea left, I took a deep breath of delight. Early in my career, I had heard a master therapist, David Treadway, speak at a professional conference. One of his take-aways stayed with me: Blood is thicker than therapy. He cautioned therapists that while developing a strong therapeutic relationship is crucial, it is only a stepping-stone that offers patients a chance to experience closeness, intimacy, and connection. What most people want is to repair their relationships with their loved ones. I wondered if experiencing my caring had given Andrea permission to access her need to be cared for.

For most of Andrea's therapy, I'd had only a shadowy picture of her mother. She had seemed to be absent, negligent, or both. But something had shifted and allowed Andrea to get in touch with her own need for connection and her mother's caring. It was as if a "good mommy" channel had opened up inside as she moved from her mother stroking her hair to comforting her after she fell off a bicycle. It was as if she was now able to access the love that had been there all along but that somehow had gone unacknowledged.

The day after our session, Andrea called her parents and arranged for a weekend visit. Later that week, she returned a telephone call to Janice, who had been her favorite cousin when they were growing up. Janice had been leaving cell phone and text messages for months. When they met, she surprised herself by confiding in her cousin about the extent of her bulimia. Her self-disclosure made her realize how rarely she opened up and expressed her real feelings to others. She was deeply entrenched in a lifelong pattern of silencing her feelings. Just recognizing this seemed to give her a push.

In the following session, Andrea told me how she had confronted her boyfriend, Ben.

"I told him I didn't care what he did but that if he didn't work, he'd have to move out. I told him if he couldn't find anything better to do, driving a cab was fine with me." To her surprise, Ben agreed. We revisited her lava rock, and she realized how her fear of confronting him had left her feeling stuck and victimized, and how her bulimia had been a heavy weight keeping her disconnected from her own needs, as well as those of others.

That afternoon, after my last patient left, I opened the door of my home office to step out on the porch to get the mail. It was unusually warm for early May, and the days were growing longer, a harbinger of the good things I associate with summer: sunny days at the beach; slow meals with company; time to vacation, read, and relax. Closing the mailbox, I caught sight of the forsythia bushes, already in bloom. The buds on the tulips and daffodils surrounding the porch were opening.

For the first time in a long time, I remembered my mother coming to visit me when I was a young mother and my children were small. I'd been so delighted when she had offered to plant my flowerbeds. How she had enjoyed engaging her grandchildren in gardening projects! She'd gotten a blue watering can for Zach and a pink one for Rachel. I remembered the Mother's Day tradition we established later on: planting tomatoes, peppers, and cucumbers in the vegetable garden in the backyard, ingredients for the gazpacho we prepared all summer long. Late that night after I remembered these things, I noticed how warmly I felt about my mother. I wondered if my session with Andrea had awakened not only her needs but my own as well.

A year later, Andrea was accepted to graduate school in her home state. She moved home and left therapy. Three months after that, I received a letter from her father: "Thank you for helping our daughter—she is a different person. We are so happy to have her home again and grateful to you for helping her."

Faye, Daughter of Lois:
Always Critical

"I woke up this morning feeling paralyzed. I must have known that I'd be getting bad news, because I was so panicky, I couldn't drive to work. Thankfully, Ron was able to take me to my office. I'm such a loser, he must be getting fed up with me," Faye said, and she began to cry.

An attractive bank manager in her mid-thirties, Faye was devastated. After a series of stressful interviews, she'd just learned that the promotion she had hoped to get had fallen through. Once again, she had been overlooked. "What's new?" she said, pushing one of her dark curls behind her ear. "I'm a loser."

I'd worked with Faye intermittently since she'd been a teenager, when an eating disorder drove her to my office; I'd heard these familiar words from her before. As the furrow between her eyebrows deepened, I remembered her lifelong history: mercilessly badgering herself with self-doubt. After overcoming her eating disorder, she was sure she wouldn't graduate from college. Next, she feared she was on the brink of a "serious" drinking problem. I reassured her that a glass or two of wine did not mean she was on the road to alcoholism, and she seemed to relax, but shortly after that, she transferred her obsessive worry and perfectionism to the project of purchasing a new car—what if she made a mistake?

Twenty years later, now married and the mother of two daughters, Faye was a stronger and more competent version of her younger self, yet she was discovering that her perfectionism and worry were infecting her parenting. The theme of her negative self-talk, emblematic of a deeper childhood wound, remained. Faye knew that managing her negative ruminations was her number one challenge, yet she often felt powerless.

Sitting in my office, Faye reviewed her failed job interview.

"Was I too quiet? Did I say the wrong thing? Did I wear the wrong suit? Was my skirt too short? My earrings too long?"

As I listened to her pick herself apart, dwelling on what she saw as her mistakes and flaws, I felt my adrenaline surge. She was on a familiar downward spiral. To let her go on berating herself felt counterproductive.

"Faye, I want to interrupt you," I said. "I'm noticing that you're caught up in an old story—beating yourself up." I hoped to remind her that she had the power to disrupt her habitual reactions. "Are you willing to do an experiment?"

She nodded.

In telling our stories, sometimes words are useless. Often we overlook the healing power of the body. Simply slowing down and paying attention to our breathing can help us regulate our emotions, calm down, and stabilize ourselves.

"Let's see what will happen if you take two deep breaths in and let them go. You may want to gently close your eyes, or, if you don't want to, it's okay to leave them open. Just breathe in deeply and out completely and notice how your body likes to breathe. Just notice your own breathing rhythm."

As I said these words to Faye, I noticed that not only was she quieting down, but so was I. Faye's face had softened; the deep line between her eyebrows was smoothed out.

"What was that like?" I asked.

"I feel calmer. I guess I needed that," she said. "How did you know?"

"I didn't know, but I noticed how much tension you hold in your face, and in your body. Our bodies matter more than we sometimes realize. Relaxing our bodies can calm our minds. I was struck by how hard you were being on yourself."

"I'm like that," Faye said. "Hard on myself. And I've always been this way. I know I drive myself; it's probably at the root of my success . . . and my distress."

"I wonder if it's something you might want to work on," I said.

To my surprise, Faye nodded yes, she would like to learn to be kinder to herself.

"What would it be like if you took two more deep breaths and allowed your body to soften?"

We spent the rest of the session alternating between practicing relaxation exercises and noticing their calming effects on her body.

After Faye left, I thought about the difficulties involved in growing up and separating ourselves from the internalized negativity we can absorb from our families. Although Faye had certainly made great strides in creating a richer life, she still easily fell back into persistent self-attacks. A story she'd told me when she began therapy, years earlier, came to mind.

"I was in first grade, and blue-and-white saddle shoes were 'in.' I really, really wanted a pair, but, knowing how tight money was in my family, I was hesitant to ask. Finally, I gathered my courage."

Her mother's tight lips should have been a warning. A clipped, tense delivery followed. "You don't need them," were Lois's words. At first, her mother was dead set against this "unnecessary" purchase, but, after much begging, Faye made headway and her mother acquiesced. Faye was thrilled to be able to wear her new saddle shoes to her best friend Rachel's birthday party.

When the party ended, her mother arrived to pick her up, scowling. "What happened?" Lois asked, looking at Faye's shoes.

Looking down, Faye shivered. Her shoes were splattered with mud. She had no idea how to respond. The party had been in Rachel's backyard, and one of the activities had been bobbing for apples. She hadn't realized how muddy the yard had gotten and that her shoes were dirty.

Faye's mother behaved herself on the car ride home, but Faye was wary because she knew why—the car was filled with other kids. Once they'd been dropped off, her mother continued the silent treatment, which for Faye was worse than being yelled at. When they got home, her mother lashed out at her. "Take off those shoes. This is how you treat your new clothes? Don't you dare ask me for anything new again! How could you be so careless?" I remember being struck at that time with how Faye had internalized her mother's criticism.

Her mother then pulled out a large box containing shoe polish and an assortment of rags. She sat her six-year-old daughter down and gave her instructions on how to "carefully" apply the white polish. But this job was far too difficult for a child that young.

"I should have known you'd mess this up," she told Faye, as she snatched the shoes away from her daughter. And thus began Faye's descent into self-contempt.

"I remember my older brother teasing me and calling me a loser," she recalled, as we unraveled how her insecurity developed, became reinforced in adolescence, and solidified into an obsession with perfectionism by adulthood. "I know I come across as tense, and I even know the reasons why," she said, staring at me. "My question is, will I ever be able to change?"

"You ask a good question," I said. "If I didn't believe change and growth are always possible, I couldn't be a therapist." I explained that we all change in different ways, and I suggested she practice incorporating some of the breathing exercises we had done into her daily life. Having a "homework assignment," she said, left her feeling hopeful.

After she left that day, I realized Faye's story had pushed my buttons. Usually that phrase indicates a wound has been triggered, but in this case, the button that got pushed was not a wound but a realization about a gift I'd been blessed with that poor Faye had not.

———

It was my forty-eighth birthday, and my family was gathered at a local Italian restaurant. My mother lifted her glass and toasted me with her signature story. Her voice was soft and lilting, her eyes sparkling.

"My Judy," she said, "always danced to her own drummer. When she was four years old, she was dying for a pair of red boots. Even as a small child, she was persistent as hell, like a dog with a bone. She nagged me to death, until, one rainy day, I gave in. The day I bought her those red boots, she was euphoric. When we were ready to leave the shoe store, she wouldn't take them off to go home—she ran out of the store with them on and then proceeded to run up and down Central Avenue, splashing in every puddle she could find. She got such a kick out of those boots!

"That night, when it was time to put on her pajamas, I couldn't get those boots off her. What a struggle she gave me! The next morning, when I got up and went into her room, no Judy. I searched the house and finally noticed the front door was wide open, so I looked outside. There she was, out on the sidewalk, riding her red tricycle." My mother paused dramatically. "You know what she was wearing? Nothing, nothing at all—just her red boots. Yup, stark naked!

"How she got outside, I have no idea. But what a scene! Judy on her red tricycle, stark naked, wearing only her red boots. Yup, that's my Judy—she always danced to her own drummer!"

Back then when she told this story, she took great glee in describing me as her feisty, high-energy daughter who loved to break rules, take chances, and dance to her own drummer. No, she wasn't embarrassed by her naked daughter riding her bicycle in the early-morning hours. In fact, I don't even remember being scolded. In all the years I heard her tell and retell this story, what I recall is her conveying how cute I was and how much she admired my reckless joy.

Growth, Healing,
and Transformation

After one of my patients faced a stressful moment at work, she left me a message I have never forgotten. "Thank you for today, Dr. Rabinor," she said. "I took you in my pocket, and you calmed me down when I had to confront my boss."

Theorists from diverse schools of thought assume that one consequence of good therapy is that patients internalize the supportive presence of the therapist. Less discussed is the fact that the therapy relationship is a crucible for the therapist's development as well. These stories demonstrate that witnessing my patients' struggles offered me endless opportunities to rethink my own growth. That healing is a never-ending process. All that is necessary are a few crucial ingredients: the capacity to cultivate and tolerate living in the unknown; taking risks; failing and starting over; and the belief that our own struggles offer us the opportunity to build new strengths and resources.

PART SIX:

Making Peace

Imagine your mother alone in a reflective moment. Maybe she stops in the middle of a daily activity, like paying bills or washing dishes, and just gazes into the middle distance or out the window. She is unaware you are watching her. What observations do you make of her in such a moment? What do you imagine preoccupies her? Is she daydreaming? What is on her mind?

Welcome to *Sally*

"Good morning, Dr. Rabinor. I'm Lilly, an assistant producer of *Sally*. We're looking for an expert for our episode, 'Mothers, Daughters, and the Battle of the Bulge.' We need someone who is TV savvy and can keep it together under pressure. I saw you run an amazing therapy group on *Oprah* last month. After watching you on the episode 'Too Ugly to Leave the House,' I knew we had to get you on *Sally*. Are you available this Friday morning?"

My heart was pounding. *Sally* was one of the most popular daytime television talk shows in the country, viewed by millions daily. Plus, Sally Jessy Raphael was a trailblazer—she was the first woman to host a live, audience-participation talk show focusing on women's issues. I had never seen the show, but I'd heard about it ad nauseam; my mother was a giant fan.

"The show will be dynamite, Dr. Rabinor. We have three pairs of mothers and daughters feuding with each other about their weight, plus all the issues that plague mothers and daughters: competition, jealousy, envy, success, and failure. We need an experienced therapist, an expert who can work with eating problems and the mother-daughter relationship."

It was 1994, and I was fifty-two years old. Mothers, daughters, and eating disorders were my niche. I had written professionally about mothering and was conducting Healing the Mother-Daughter Relationship workshops all over the country. Appearing as a TV therapist on Oprah's "Too Ugly to Leave the House" had brought me more attention and fame than I had ever expected. I had been inundated with invitations for book contracts, interviews, and appearances on news and talk shows.

I was at an incredible moment in my life. My career was soaring. I had a long waiting list of new patients. Professional opportunities abounded. The heavy lifting of parenthood was over: Rachel, my youngest child, was off to the University of Colorado in Boulder, and my son, Zach, had just graduated from Cornell. Almost all the balls were in the air, except one: I had been divorced for more than a decade and was still on the lookout for Mr. Right.

I got off the phone with Sally Jessy's assistant and immediately called my mother. "Guess what, Ma? I'm going to be on the *Sally* show on Friday! Wanna come with me? It's being taped right here in New York City, on West Fifty-Seventh Street. A limo is picking me up at eight in the morning. We can stop at your apartment and get you on the way to the studio."

"Sally Jessy Raphael!" my mother exclaimed. "I can't believe it! I wouldn't miss this for the world!"

"I know it's early for you, Ma. You sure?"

"Not over my dead body would I miss this!"

I can't believe it. There goes my mother—she's strung two clichés together in less than a minute. Okay, okay, I know: I'm being picky, like a snippy teenager, criticizing her.

Even though I had invited her to come with me and was thrilled she had accepted, she was already annoying me. I had to admit it—while she could be irritating, she could also be comforting. And I was nervous. Being on TV as an expert is daunting, and this *Sally* show was going to be a challenge. *Oprah* was a taped show, with the possibility of editing out any glaring errors I might make, whereas *Sally* would be live. Whatever happened in the studio would be immediately visible to millions in the TV audience. Having my mother there might help me stay calm.

"I'll call you later, Ma."

"Don't hang up, honey—get your hair done on Thursday, please! And what are you going to wear? I know what a big moment this is for you. I'm having lunch at Bergdorf's today; they're running a sale." She paused, and when she spoke, her voice was low, a bit tentative. "You're not going to wear that pink jacket you wore on *Oprah*, are you? That was a mistake—pink is not a flattering color for you. Maybe I can pick something up for you. If you don't like it, I'll return it."

My head began to spin. "Gotta get off now, Ma," I said, biting my tongue. *I can't believe her.* A dull pain in my belly was growing. A familiar wave of nausea was spreading. I realized how absurd it was that I had been asked to be an expert about the mother-daughter relationship and had invited my own mother, and now that she was coming to the show, she was what was making me most anxious.

Why have I done this to myself again? I pulled my mother into my world and then, almost instantaneously, was filled with fear and regret. I should have been able to accept this push-pull dynamic I saw in my office every day: mothers and daughters coming in and bickering with each other while longing to be close. I tried to help them recognize the complexity of intimacy. I often repeated my favorite C. G. Jung quote: "Every mother contains her daughter in herself and every daughter her mother and every mother extends backwards into her mother and forwards into her daughter."

"Closeness is complex," I would say, reminding my patients (and myself) that throughout time, poets, writers, and thinkers have described the mother-daughter dynamic as one of the most intense, beautiful, and difficult of all relationships.

I felt my breath quicken as I thought about my mother. I was deeply attached and devoted to her—that, I knew. Perhaps one problem I had was acknowledging that attachment always involves some ambivalence. Healthy ambivalence helps a child separate from the parents, yet accepting my own ambivalence toward my mother was not easy. During my doctoral program, I wrote my dissertation on the topic of attachment. I learned that the attachment styles we develop in childhood become blueprints for relationships throughout the human life cycle.

I had never had trouble finding boyfriends or making friends, which made me realize that perhaps my attachment to my mother was "good enough." However, I was aware that although I was attached to her, I knew how to keep my distance. I had created my own strategies of disconnection, such as belittling her concrete, non-reflective, non-introspective style. However, whenever I heard myself belittle my mother, I saw how quickly I felt uncomfortable and ran to her defense by focusing, at least in my mind, on her strengths. She brought her optimism and sense of humor to everything she did. She knew how to cope calmly with disaster and loss. For example, after Lenny, her second husband, died, she returned to college—at fifty-five! When I first heard her talking about going back to school, I had had my doubts that she'd follow through with it, but, to my surprise, she did. She not only survived but thrived, earning a Bachelors in Social Work from Fordham University when she was sixty-three.

Yes, my mother could be a paragon of practicality and resilience, but sometimes when I thought of her, I got in touch with an icy edge deep within me. I couldn't—or wouldn't— let go of some of the ways in which she had deceived me. I carried a couple of big grudges. She had been selfish and insensitive. She had behaved hurtfully, over and over, and although I wanted to forgive her, there were entrenched memories that lingered. I had discussed them in therapy and written about them for decades. She had apologized, but her words always sounded hollow, meant only to appease me. She still had no idea why I felt injured and she never truly sounded remorseful. Every time I brought up her insincere apologies, old wounds were pricked open and I became hurt and angry again. And on top of that, I couldn't forgive myself for not being able to let go of my feelings. Her betrayals still nagged at me, but we had gone over them a hundred times, to no avail. Now, because I had nothing new to say about them, I picked at little things instead, and they grew into big things.

I hated myself when I criticized her, because when I had been in trouble, she had been there for me, at least sometimes. When I lost my fiancé at twenty-four, it was my mother who dropped everything to go to the funeral with me. Since my divorce, she had been generous to my children and me, with her time, love, and money. Yet the critical part of me kicked in whenever an old wound was triggered.

Now, as I contemplated my "expert" TV appearance, new worries cropped up. *My mother will be sitting in the audience. What if Sally sees her and invites her up on the stage? What if Sally asks me personal questions about how I've navigated our relationship? Or, worse, what if she asks my mother? Who knows what my mother will say? She could start talking about our wonderful relationship, and I might easily become unglued.*

As I contemplated all the ways in which a live interview could go wrong, my head began pounding. Several of my patients, I realized, watched *Sally* regularly. Another worry: I might not know how to answer a question Sally posed. I might sound like a complete idiot. And if I did really well, who knew how that might impact my therapy relationship with my clients? Seeing me in the limelight could evoke envy in some patients, who, unable to own competitive feelings, might then elect to leave therapy.

My mind continued to race. I glanced at my appointment book and saw that after the show, I was scheduled to have five sessions back to back, starting at 2:00 p.m. All but one involved an enmeshed mother-daughter relationship. *Who am I to give advice?* Looking at my appointment book, I started to sweat.

That Friday morning, when we arrived at Sally Jessy Raphael's studio, the place was abuzz with energy. After the makeup artist and hair stylist worked their magic, I was transformed: not a wrinkle visible or a hair out of place.

Finally, we were in the Green Room. My anxiety mounted.

"You'll be great, honey," my mother reminded me. Suddenly, the door flew open and I was whisked onto the stage. Until this moment, I had not had a glimpse of Sally or of any of the mother-daughter couples I was about to meet.

Wearing her signature oversize, red-rimmed glasses, Sally introduced the three "food-bonded" mother-daughter duos sitting on the stage, one by one, to the audience and me.

"These mothers and daughters are obsessed with dieting, losing weight, and what they weigh. They pick on each other day and night, mercilessly, about what to eat and each other's weight." Sally paused dramatically and then turned to me. "Today, we have Dr. Judy Rabinor with us. She's a psychologist who specializes in weight problems and is an expert on the mother-daughter relationship. She runs workshops helping mothers and daughters make peace with one another. Judy," she said, "Is weight really the issue, or is there something else going on here?"

"Great question, Sally," I said, knowing intuitively I must start off by engaging the audience where they lived—in their hearts. "Here, we have three pairs of mothers and daughters talking nonstop about food, weight, and dieting, and they are not alone. Mothers and daughters everywhere get caught up in 'fat talk.' After all, we live in a weight-obsessed culture." I paused and peered into the studio audience, filled with women, with what I hoped was a look of compassion. "I see from the nods in the audience that what you eat and what you weigh grip most of you, too."

A low murmur of confirmation from the audience validated me.

"So how," Sally continued, "do we find out what their real issues are?"

Rather than give a mini-lecture, I decided to engage the audience directly. "I have an exercise for us to do together. It's not just for the mothers or the daughters up here on the stage with me. I think everyone here might learn something about themselves, because obsessing about food and weight is a cultural epidemic. The television audience can join in and do this exercise, too."

I paused. "I'd like everyone to take a slow breath in and let it go. Inhale deeply and exhale completely. You may want to close your eyes . . ." I leaned back in my chair and breathed deeply as I began to lead the audience in one of my favorite guided-imagery exercises. "Take another deep breath in, then let it go. Inhale deeply and exhale completely. Imagine you're in a place that is calm and relaxing. You may be on your living room couch or your bed. You may be outdoors, sitting on a beach, in the woods, or in your own backyard. Take another deep breath in, and let it go. Inhale deeply, exhale completely. And now," I said, after what I hoped was a dramatic pause, "imagine you have just inhaled a special gas with magical powers. When you breathe in this gas, your weight will never change. Take another deep breath in, and as you let it go, digest the fact that you have just inhaled a very special gas and your weight will never change. It doesn't matter if you eat pizza and cannolis or carrots and celery, if you starve or binge, if you exercise all day or never exercise. The weight you are now, at this moment, is the weight you will be forever."

At this point, the camera scanned the studio. The entire audience, as well as the three mother-daughter pairs, were all in a light trance.

"In a moment, I'm going to ask all of you to open your eyes," I continued, "but before you do that, take a moment to notice what it feels like inside to imagine your weight is never going to change." I wanted to demonstrate the power of the imagination, generally an undervalued tool.

A moment later, I asked everyone to open their eyes.

"Where's that gas?" Sally asked, with a big smile. "I want it now!"

When the laughter from the audience died down, I turned to the pair on the stage sitting closest to me: Robin, a pretty, twentysomething daughter; and Sandy, her mother, who was wearing an oversize housedress. When, at the beginning of the show, Sally had introduced them as "once both overweight," Robin had interrupted her.

"Now that I've lost fifty pounds, my mom is jealous of me." Robin had sneered at her mother. Her big brown eyes flashed as she spoke loudly. She was wearing tight red slacks and a revealing black V-neck sweater.

"Robin and Sandy," I said, "what is it like to live in a world where your weight will never change, where now it doesn't matter what you eat, because you will never lose or gain weight? What are you going to talk about now that food, weight, and fat talk are off-limits?"

"We can't talk about our weight?" Robin asked.

"Nope." I shook my head. "Weight is off-limits!"

To my surprise, Sandy turned to her daughter and said, "We're going to have to deal with each other. With other things."

"Other things?" I asked.

Sandy looked at me blankly.

"What do you want to say to your daughter? What do you want to deal with?"

Another blank look greeted me. Both mother and daughter were silent. I had a moment of anxiety.

"Let's see," I said, buying myself some time to think. "We could start with what prompted you to come to this program about the battle between mothers and daughters," I suggested.

Sandy jumped in. "I truly love Robin, but this fat thing—"

"Wait a minute," I said. "Remember, we're not going to talk about food or weight. But you started to say something important: You truly love Robin."

Sandy stared hard at me. "Robin is very smart; she's a good mother; she's clean, kind, and considerate; and she's a hard worker." She spoke in a strong voice.

"Sandy," I said softly, "can you say that directly to your daughter, Robin?"

Sandy turned to her daughter. She looked directly at her and smiled. When she began speaking, her voice dropped. "Robin, it's true. You are a good mother; you're smart and kind and considerate."

Robin's mouth had fallen open. "You look stunned," I said to her. She nodded. "When is the last time your mother told you that you are smart, considerate, and a good mother?"

"Not in a long time," she said, after a pause.

I was amazed. In less than a minute, the energy between this mother and daughter had shifted visibly. I was determined to expand and explore this healing moment. Although often therapy is aimed at helping mothers and daughters express their anger toward one another, I had already discovered that it is not the inability to express anger that limits growth, but the inability to express love and caring.

"Tell your mom how it makes you feel when you hear her say these words," I suggested to Robin.

"It makes me feel good about myself," Robin said.

"So, let's take a moment and pause. Let's think about how this kind of talk happened here today—and how maybe it can happen more often."

"It doesn't happen," Sandy said, "because we're usually too busy talking about who eats what and who shouldn't be eating this or that!"

"We're too busy talking about who's fat and who's thin!" Robin chimed in.

I paused, wanting Robin and Sandy to absorb the enormity of this moment—there are other things that are important to talk about besides food and weight. I didn't want to come across as too preachy or heavy. "I guess the secret is to keep away from talking about food and weight!" I said playfully.

In a thoughtful voice, Sandy continued, "Robin's too busy looking at what I'm eating. Our weight and our eating get all the attention!"

I lowered my voice. "Sandy, what do you think your daughter would really like to get attention for?"

Robin turned to me. "I'd like attention for who I really am on the inside: a good mother; a smart, considerate person."

"Can you tell your mother that?" I asked Robin.

Robin turned to Sandy and repeated herself. "I'd like attention for who I really am on the inside."

The room was silent.

"Where did you learn to be a good mother? A smart, considerate person?" I asked Robin.

Robin giggled and, for the first time, beamed at her mother. "I learned all this from my mother."

In just a minute or two, caring smiles and warmth had replaced the angry, sneering energy between this mother and daughter. When she was "forbidden" to talk about food, weight, and fat, another side of Sandy emerged: a mother who admired her daughter. A new cycle had been activated. In response to Sandy's genuine admiration for her daughter, a transformed Robin had expressed a deep appreciation of her mother.

Witnessing this transformation blew me away. Much of my psychotherapy training had taught me that expressing pent-up hostility is what heals, but before my eyes, I was witnessing the opposite. Expressing hostility often escalates to a damaging vicious cycle, while expressing admiration seems to yield what Sandy and Robin wanted—appreciation and love. I was of course familiar with this cycle. A kind word from a boyfriend generally evoked a tender response on my own part, while nastiness begat nastiness. Perhaps the inability to express love is what limits growth. Perhaps what people really want—or need—is permission to express pent-up love.

At that moment, the camera panned out across the studio audience.

"Are you all right?" Sally had bent down to address an audience participant whose face was hidden from my view. As Sally moved slightly and altered her position, I got a glimpse of the bent head of a tearful woman. I found myself gasping. The person she was speaking to wore a familiar tweed herringbone jacket and a beige silk scarf.... *Wait a minute—that's the scarf I bought my mother for her birthday!*

Sally was talking to my mother! What was my mother doing in the audience? I had left her in the Green Room, but now she was sitting right there and Sally had zeroed in on her.

My mother was sniffling. Sally moved in closer, and my mother's face became visible. Tearfully she said, "I'm really fine, just fine."

"You're saying you're fine, but you're crying!" Sally said warmly. "You don't seem so fine."

I was incredulous. Here was my tearful mother, denying she was crying! This was one thing about her that I could never understand. My mother could not acknowledge that either she or I might be emotional. It had taken me years of

psychotherapy to understand how growing up in an atmosphere where denial of pain was the norm damaged my own
psychological development and caused me to feel shame about
expressing my feelings. And here was my mother, denying her
obvious, tearful reaction!

My mother mumbled something unintelligible, and Sally
swooped in. "Is it because of the mother-daughter relationship?" Sally asked.

My mother nodded. "What Dr. Rabinor said to these girls
is beautiful. How she's helped them."

Yeah, Ma! I wanted to scream out. She looked so touched,
and emotionally responsive in a way I'd never seen her. Her
voice was filled with depth and emotion as she and Sally gazed
at each other. And she was handling herself perfectly. Thankfully, she hadn't blown it and identified herself as my mother.

As the camera zoomed back in on me, I felt my stomach soften. In this moment, I realized why I had invited my
mother to come with me. It wasn't just that she could be comforting. She could, but there was more. I had longed for her to
see me and know who I was and what I believed in. I wanted
her to see that genuine emotional connections are healing. I
wanted her to know how being a therapist had enriched my
life. And I wanted her to see how far I had come and how
different I was from her.

"Well, Dr. Rabinor," Sally said, turning back to me and
interrupting my reverie, "Where do we go from here?"

Lunch at the Paris Bistro

We were seated at a small table in the rear of the Paris Bistro, a quaint French restaurant around the corner from the ABC network. My mother had insisted on celebrating what she called my "mah-velous" performance. She had used this word a dozen times, but I had let it be; now, the bottle of pinot grigio she had ordered was sitting squarely on a white plate on the red-and-white-checkered tablecloth.

"Congratulations! You really knew how to handle those mothers and daughters," she told me, for what must have been the tenth time, as we clinked our glasses. "You were just marvelous!" She had been overflowing with accolades as we reviewed the show blow by blow. She was obviously astute and had picked up the nuances of several interchanges, but something left me wary. Eventually, we turned to Sally's serendipitous focus on my mother.

"Do you think she knew I was your mother?" she asked.

"I don't think so, and, in any event, it doesn't matter. You were terrific, Mom. You were just mah-velous." I exaggerated her pronunciation, and we both began giggling. She knew I was imitating her, but it was fine, because I did so with love. I reassured her that it really didn't matter if Sally knew she was my mother, because what was most important was that my mother had called attention to my skill as a therapist.

"You did a great job, Mom. You showed how touched you were by the work I did with Sandy and Robin. People watch television to be emotionally moved, and your tears were an endorsement of the work I did enabling that mother and daughter to connect on a deeper level. They stopped picking on each other and got in touch with their genuine positive feelings. And that's what Sally is really all about—helping people get in touch with their emotional core. Not only did they change, but you, an audience member, were clearly genuinely moved!"

"Good, dear, good. I'm so glad you invited me. It was really something to see you up there with Sally! My daughter onstage with *the* Sally Jessy Raphael."

I was aware that I was beginning to deflate. My mother was talking but not really responding to me—I was feeling invisible. Had she not heard me? Was it not possible for her to focus on what I was saying? It didn't take me long to realize that something paradoxical was going on. I had pushed Robin and Sandy to go deeper, but I was having trouble doing that in my own life. I realized that my mother was moving into an unreachable mode and that if things were to change, I must push myself. I must do for myself what I had done for Robin and Sandy. I must take a risk.

"I never see you cry, Mom. Never! So it really surprised me." My mother shrugged, but I was determined to push on. "Tell me, Mom, what made you get so tearful?"

"I don't know. Was it bad that I was crying?" she asked.

Her response seemed odd. How could crying be "bad"? "Not at all, Mom. But I'm curious about what it was that touched you."

"I don't really remember," she said, "but as long as my crying wasn't a problem for you, I'm fine."

With that, a memory from my office arose.

Beth was a twenty-six-year-old elementary-school teacher who suffered deep shame if she ever cried. I attempted to explain that tears were our inborn mechanism of self-soothing. My explanation fell on deaf ears. We spoke of Beth's tears and her shame about them, to no avail. How, I wondered, could I help her appreciate that her tears were an expression of her genuine emotional depth?

To my surprise, one day Beth came in and told me she'd attended a spiritual retreat and heard a story she wanted to share.

When Adam and Eve were driven out of the Garden of Eden, they were forced into a world of trauma and grief that defied description.
God took pity upon them.
"My children," he said, "life is full of pain, and I want to bestow upon you my most precious gift." He handed them a pearl. "This pearl symbolizes tears. When you are overwhelmed by grief, if you allow tears to fall from your eyes, your burden will be easier to bear."
With these words, Adam and Eve let out their grief. Tears poured from their eyes and moistened the earth. The story left a precious inheritance: When someone is in great grief, if they permit their tears to flow, their grief will ease. The simple lesson is that going into one's pain eases grief.

I was determined not to give up on my mother. I said, "I so appreciated your tears, your genuine reaction, your recognition of how those mothers and daughters had love for one another."

"Yes, you did a good job at getting them to open up."

"Mom, I realize how touched I was to see you cry, and that you never cry."

"I know that's true," she said. "I'm just not a crier."

I felt my heart racing. *Help her be curious,* I reminded myself, *just like you do with patients.*

"I've never understood this about you, Ma. You didn't cry when you called to tell me Dad was terminal. Or when Lenny died. Or when Herbert died. Or when Michael died. Those times—when I was so sad—I remember thinking, *Why isn't my mother crying?* You were just carrying on, Ma. Do you know what I'm talking about?"

"I don't really know what's bothering you, Judy," she said, and I sensed she was becoming defensive. "Of course I was sad, but when I'm sad, I can carry on. There are some people who just take to their bed; I'm not one of them. All those losses were terrible, and they were all in January, too. It's not my favorite month; it's the month I dread most in the entire year. Every year when January comes along, I think, *The month of losses is here.* But I carry on. Usually I get theater tickets or something to keep me busy, to keep my mind off what happened."

At that moment, the waiter arrived with the bill and our conversation shifted, but my thoughts about my mother lingered. It had taken me a long time to understand that my mother constructed her life to avoid pain and that doing so made perfect sense to her. Although I didn't understand exactly why, I realized I would have to accept our differences. While ordering theater tickets wasn't my way of dealing with my feelings, keeping busy in this way seemed to work for her.

Only later would I realize that I had developed my own ways of escaping pain. Only later would I realize that just six months after my father's death I enrolled in a PhD program. Certainly, with an active toddler, I must have unconsciously known attending graduate school would keep me busy and might allow me to stave off my grief about the loss of my father, my resentment about my mother's affair, and my deteriorating relationship with my husband. It would take me a while to dig down deeper.

Celebrating Life in
the Shadow of Death

It was early 1998 when, unexpectedly, a window on my past opened up. My mother's eightieth birthday was approaching that April; a celebration was called for, but we were a family in mourning. My brother's wife, Shira, had died suddenly, at fifty-three; it had been only months from a terminal cancer diagnosis to the raw day in January when we lowered her casket into the frozen earth. To celebrate while my brother, their children, and Shira's parents were buried in deep mourning felt cruel. How could we honor longevity in the midst of grieving Shira—wife, mother, daughter, sister, friend, soon-to-be grandmother—now gone? Yet ignoring the blessings of my mother's long life also seemed unacceptable.

Newly remarried after thirteen years of being a single parent, I was settling into married life with Larry, my new husband. One part of me thrived—feeling loved, loving, and settled was a gift—while another part of me seemed to be withering. While I watered my plants, fed my cats, saw my patients, and wept for Shira, John, and our extended family, T. S. Eliot's words from *The Waste Land* hummed in my mind:

April is the cruelest month, breeding
Lilacs out of the dead land, mixing
Memory and desire, stirring
Dull roots with spring rain.

I felt like I was in a fog. I had trouble getting out of bed in the morning. My appetite disappeared. I lost weight and was plagued by lethargy. It didn't take long before I realized I'd been pulled into a well of grief. At twenty-four, I had lost my fiancé in a fatal car accident. When I was thirty, my father was suddenly gone. At forty, I'd divorced. Shira's loss pricked not only at old pain but at new fears. At fifty-four, I was the age my father had been when he died. Perhaps, I realized, I had never mourned him. Perhaps my unmourned losses had been in hiding, waiting silently for this moment.

In the midst of my fog, I welcomed sitting with my patients and digging down deep. Emotional processing, the bedrock of my workday as a therapist, was where I needed to be. Emotional processing means helping people know and be with what is on their minds and in their hearts. Processing implies movement; disturbing emotions can soften when we speak about them with an empathic listener. Processing implies that things are always changing; what we feel at one moment is not necessarily what we will feel at another. Processing implies the possibility of growth and renewal. It may seem ironic, but processing my patients' wounds was personally helpful.

I recalled the words of a graduate school professor: "Mourning begets mourning." He urged us to courageously help our patients take the time to grieve the inevitable losses that accompany every life and that often resurface with the passage of time. To my surprise, I found myself grieving my father, decades after I had lost him.

I repeatedly began seeing images of him: as a small boy; as a young man in love with my mother; as a father who taught me to ski and play tennis, gifted me with a love of opera, and walked me down the aisle. As the loss of my father came into focus, so did the realization that my obsession with discovering my mother's lover's identity had interfered with mourning my father in the aftermath of his death.

A month or two after my father died, my mother had invited my father's mother, Grandma Sophie, over for Shabbat dinner. I can still see my grandmother, dressed in black, sitting at our dining room table, tearfully sifting through photographs of bygone days, mourning my father, her youngest son. I can still see her sniffling, blowing her nose. I can still see my mother scurrying in and out of the dining room, bringing platters and condiments, clearing dishes and glasses, and preparing for dessert. What I see but don't want to see is what isn't there. In this moment, my mother and I are not crying, but we are lovingly comforting my grandmother.

I did not realize then that in the aftermath of my father's death, I'd been pulled into a destructive triangle. Thinking back, I wonder how I managed to juggle my feelings. On the one hand, I was my mother's ally, listening to her complaints about my father. On the other hand, whenever I thought about Mr. Affair, my father's face would appear and I would feel like strangling her. Now I see how my Nancy Drew obsession served a hidden purpose. It distracted me from what may have been too difficult: the work of mourning my father.

I thought of the night before I'd left for my freshman year of college at the University of Vermont, when I felt particularly close to my father. My mom was clearing the table while my dad and I finished up my favorite dessert, chocolate mousse, which my mom had made for this special occasion—I was the first in our family to go to college.

My father cleared his throat and turned to me. The blue of his eyes reminded me of a cloudless sky.

"Be careful up there at the University of Vermont," he said. "You never know what's going to happen on those cold winter nights. Don't do anything I wouldn't do."

At first, I did not know what he was talking about. What wouldn't he do? And why did his voice sound hoarse, as if he was straining or maybe nervous? Laden with dishes, my mother looked away and walked back into the kitchen, but from the way my father looked at me, I sensed there was more to be said.

We were alone at the table. My father cleared his throat a few more times before mumbling something about how a pretty girl like me would have lots of opportunities with boys. When he repeated that silly phrase a second time and added, "And a boy might sweep you off your feet," I felt a pit in my stomach. I already knew what that was like.

He cleared his throat. "Be careful, honey, very careful," he said, "and I want to tell you, in case your mother hasn't told you: Being careful means always using protection. Always use birth control."

My face felt like it was on fire. Did he think I was an idiot, unfamiliar with the "protection" euphemism? I was still a virgin and had no interest in discussing this topic with my father. My mother had never mentioned birth control, so his bringing it up seemed awkward but brave.

"We have something we want to tell you," he said.

By now, my mother had returned to the dining room table. "More chocolate mousse, anyone?" she asked cheerfully.

"Peggy, sit down," my father said. His voice sounded cracked. "I'm telling Judy how we eloped because we weren't careful."

I stared at them in disbelief. My mother sat silently, smiling. My father did all the talking. They hadn't gotten to go to college because my mom had gotten pregnant and they had to get married.

"You had to get married?" I asked. Having to marry was, I knew, shameful.

He nodded yes, which was why he wanted to warn me that I should avoid getting "in trouble." I'd never heard my dad sound this real, this sensitive. They'd paid a heavy price, he explained. Instead of going to college, they went to a justice of the peace in a little town on Long Island, just the two of them. No big, fancy wedding, no wedding dress, no honeymoon, and no college.

"You got married alone? Your parents didn't come to your wedding?" This was a lot for me to digest at seventeen.

"Nope. Just the two of us. We eloped. Two eighteen-year-old lovebirds waiting for a baby." My dad's eyes were full. He sounded so quiet, so sensitive.

"Were your parents mad at you?"

At first, neither of them responded. "I think they were disappointed in us," my dad said finally. What I remember now is the look in his blue eyes: sad and troubled. I had never heard my father talk about mistakes. He always seemed to be so sure of himself. This was not the bossy, domineering, and always-so-certain father I knew. His voice was low, soft, and vulnerable as he repeated the phrase "a costly mistake," then added, "That's why we're telling you—because we care."

One of the things I have loved most about being married was drinking coffee together while we both got ready for the day. Family—spouses, parents, children—offers a unique sense of comfort and continuity. That's what I had with my father. If he wasn't on the front lawn, picking crabgrass, he'd be in the living room, the opera on the stereo turned up just a bit too loud. His presence permeated my world.

As I processed the loss of my father, my sense of lethargy diminished and my energy returned. Although I didn't really understand how or why, by the time my mother's birthday arrived, I was more ready, or at least more able, to celebrate her.

Welcome to Peggy's Eightieth Birthday Party

About thirty-five guests were gathered in my living room. We began with a simple candle-lighting ritual, celebrating life, hope, and my mother. We lit a special candle to invite Shira's departed soul into the room and recalled her unique energy. We lit other candles in memory of my father; my mother's deceased husband Lenny; Herbert, her partner of many years; her parents; and other close relatives. I felt as if we were sitting with ghosts. We offered a goblet of water to my mother, along with a blessing of gratitude for the elements that sustain life: the air we breathe, the water we drink, and the life force a close family offers, especially in times of loss.

The centerpiece of the ceremony was a guided-imagery meditation I created to involve everyone. As I led the group, my mother sat with her eyes closed, head tilted, hands clasped in her lap, dressed in a beige silk pantsuit. Smiling, she looked relaxed and beautiful.

"Take a few deep breaths," I said. "Inhale deeply, exhale completely. If you like, allow your eyes to gently close as you go to the place where breathing in meets breathing out. Allow your mind to travel back in time to when you first met Peggy. If you have trouble recalling the first time, allow your mind to wander and soak in your memories of your relationship with her, and allow a moment of connection to emerge. It might be decades ago, or as recently as last week. Make contact with a moment that says something important to you about your relationship with my mother. Go down deep as you get a sense of what it means to you to be connected to her. Allow yourself to get in touch with who she is in your life; who she may have been in years past; the life you shared; the feelings that arise as you recall your connection; and what you feel now, in this room, with all of us together. What particular qualities in her call out to you, touch you, connect you with her and with parts of yourself?

"Memories bind us, one to another.

"Memories connect us to ourselves.

"Memories bridge past and present.

"We are our memories."

The most moving parts of this birthday ceremony were the spontaneous memories that friends and family offered after the meditation. One guest spoke of meeting Peggy as a toddler. Another met her at a PTA meeting. Others remembered her as a business-school student, a Girl Scout leader, a garden club president, and a civil rights activist. One woman brought a sixty-three-year-old photograph of Peggy and two other guests, taken at Camp Fernwood in Maine the summer of 1935. Peggy was described as "flirty at thirty, naughty at forty, nifty at fifty, and a trouper at sixty."

These tributes were eye-openers to some of the younger generation (my children, niece, and nephew), offering a new window on their grandmother's strengths, struggles, resiliency, and legacy. The contributors' voices were a moving reminder of the power that the bonds of relationship offer.

My mother seemed delighted with the accolades. Her smile was wide but her eyes, dry. I myself was tearful; I knew if I had been the recipient of these memories, I would have been weeping. It was yet another moment to notice our different styles.

Finally, my mother took the floor. She had a piece of paper in her hands, but she didn't use it. She spoke from the heart, without a note.

"How does it feel to be eighty? Just one day older. Suddenly everyone is helping me to cross the street, worrying about me. Telling me to sit down, take it easy. People keep asking me how I feel. I feel just fine! I have had a great life, with good health, loving parents, the most wonderful children and grandchildren, a close family, and good friends. Every five years since I turned sixty, my children have thrown a party to celebrate the occasion. This year, I didn't want a party because we lost Shira in January. We were all grieving. She was a beautiful, special person. But John said, 'It's your eightieth birthday. We must recognize it.' So I want to thank you all for coming!"

After the party was over, my mother's words lingered. Were we really "the most wonderful" children? And had she really had "loving" parents? Or had she made a pact to live by the intention, "Speak only good of those you love"? Although I realized I might never understand that decision, I was coming to grips with how different we were. For whatever reason, she needed to idealize all aspects of her life—and it seemed to work well enough for her.

Grit

It was just after nine in the morning on September 11, 2001. My eighty-three-year-old mother was the first person to call me.

"Turn on the TV," she said, and we sat on the phone together, terrified, horrified, mesmerized, stunned, watching the cement exploding and disintegrating into particles of sand—and then the second building fell. Were we under attack? At war? What would be next?

"Mom, I have to call Larry and find out how he is," I said.

After speaking to my husband, who was in New York City, I called my mother back. By then we knew about the terrorist attacks.

"Mom," I said, "today's your appointment, right?" Over the past couple of years, my mother's walking had deteriorated to a slow shuffle, and I had pushed her to make an appointment with a neurologist to get it checked out.

"It's today. Do you think I should go?" she asked.

"What do you want to do?"

She said, "I want to go."

You are gutsy! I thought. "Go," I said. "And call me when you get home."

That was at ten o'clock. By eleven, the world was infected with terror. Government agencies, schools, businesses small and large were closing. "Go home; be safe" was the message. My office was chaotic. Some patients canceled to stay at home with little ones; others came in numb and dumb and needing to collapse and find comfort. I tried my best to create safety in an unsafe universe. The world as we had known it had ceased to exist. New York City was locked down, and there were only unanswered questions. I was besieged with calls from worried friends and family from all over the country.

I began calling my mother at noon. One, two, three o'clock. No answer. Four o'clock. No answer. *Mom, where are you?* I left messages, called again and again. Finally, a little after five o'clock, my phone rang.

"I just got home," my mom said. "There were no taxis, so when I got out of Mount Sinai, I took a bus down Fifth Avenue, and then I walked across town."

"You *what*? You walked across town? From Fifth to York Avenues—eight long blocks? How did you do that, Ma?"

"That's why it took me so long," she said. "You know I can't walk so well."

"How did you do it?" I repeated.

"I took my time," she said. "I walked slowly. I'd walk a block and then sit down on the curb, and you know what? People were so nice. They helped me sit down; they helped me stand up; they helped me cross the street." She was tapping into one of her signature beliefs—if you reach out, you will find that life is full of opportunity.

"And what did the doctor say?" I finally asked, after I absorbed the enormity of her inner strength.

She barely skipped a beat. "He said I have Parkinson's disease."

Parkinson's would be a turning point, not only for my mother but also for our relationship. Initially, she seemed immune to the ramifications of this diagnosis. "So far, I'm fine," she said repeatedly in the year following her diagnosis. She coped with this new situation in the same way she dealt with so many other unexpected hardships in her life—with matter-of-fact practicality and optimism.

I, on the other hand, was worried, if not panicked. The little I knew of Parkinson's was not good. I had so many questions. There was no one with Parkinson's in our family—where could this have come from? How did Parkinson's progress? Was it hereditary, and, if so, was I vulnerable? What I learned in my online search scared me but ultimately prepared me for what would follow.

There is no known cause for Parkinson's disease (PD), a progressive, degenerative, neurological disorder. While it can initially be mild, it gets worse over time. The symptoms include tremors, muscle cramps, stiffness, loss of balance, and slow movement. My mother's shuffling and slowness were what had initially aroused my and my brother's concern. My research confirmed that she'd probably been struggling with a mild form of the disease for a couple of years.

At first, my mother expressed no worry, panic, or self-pity, but within a year of her diagnosis, as her symptoms worsened, her mood dropped. While she rarely complained, a grimness settled in, emotionally and physically. Her increased rigidity and stiffness interfered with her ability to walk, move, dress, shower, and cook for herself. Although at first she balked, eventually we hired a full-time aide to be her companion. Her world grew smaller.

The next stage of deterioration ushered in new difficulties. The hallmark feature of PD is the progressive loss of motor control, not only of major limbs but also of the finer muscles in the hands, mouth, and face. Within a short time, my mother's ability to control the finer muscle movements in her face disappeared. Without the ability to blink and smile, she was frequently expressionless. Her face often took on a masklike quality. The mother I knew was disappearing.

The loss of her facial expressiveness opened my eyes to something I'd never appreciated and told me something about the nature of our bond. I'd never paid much attention to the fact that my mother lit up when she saw me, but once that spark disappeared, I realized its importance. As a therapist, I knew the power of eye contact. So often, I encouraged supervisees to notice and acknowledge the healing power of the "gleam" in the mother's—or the therapist's—eye. An empathic nod or smile was sometimes the crucial ingredient when it came to creating a healing environment. But now, the gleam in my mother's eye was gone, replaced by a blank stare. Even though I was aware that it had disappeared through no fault of her own, this development ushered in a new loss. For me, who had always wanted to feel known and seen on a deeper level, I had to learn to live with the absence of her gleam. Even though I knew her "masked face" was symptomatic of the degenerative nature of PD, it now often reminded me of moments when I'd felt ignored, neglected, or simply out of sync with her.

Shoebox Therapy

My mother's precipitous plunge into mental and physical deterioration unbalanced me. Scared me. Enraged me. Pushed me into a rabbit hole of sadness. All of it. Finding ways to connect with her became more difficult as she unraveled and shut down, physically and emotionally. I found myself scrambling.

One day, I decided to clean out my mother's closet. In retrospect, I realized that act wasn't only about getting rid of the excess clothing she hadn't worn in ages; it was also a ritual. This was the way she had showed me love and care, and now I was speaking her language and caring for her. Cleaning out her closet was a legacy that had a special meaning. It was making room for the new by discarding what was no longer needed.

I came upon a Salvatore Ferragamo shoebox containing a pair of expensive snakeskin high heels she hadn't worn for years. My mother was sitting in the quilted rocking chair in her bedroom while I was organizing the pile of clothing and shoes for the Salvation Army.

"What do you think, Ma—are these for the giveaway pile?"

"They were very expensive," she said. "Very," recalling the excitement she'd felt at the Bergdorf Goodman sale when she'd found them. "Very expensive shoes are for you, dear, not the Salvation Army. Take them. I think we still wear the same size."

The shoes didn't fit me, and they wound up in the give-away pile, but the shoebox—it was sturdy, with a bright Ferragamo label—turned out to be unexpectedly useful.

I began filling the box with photographs of my newborn grandchild, Sammy. Looking at his adorable pictures, I hoped, might give me a way to reach her, bring us something fresh and life-affirming to talk about. I was correct. Sammy seemed to register—sometimes—and when he didn't, perhaps my enthusiasm about him was enough to keep both of us smiling. I began bringing other photos to my mother's apartment, and before long, the box was crammed.

Digging into the jumble, I could always find something to talk about.

"Look at this hat your mother was wearing," I'd say, handing her an ancient tinted photo of her parents, the grandparents I adored, Grandma Lillian and Grandpa Henry, sitting side by side, dressed in their finery, holding hands. My grandmother was wearing a beaded dress and a stylish cloche hat with a small feather sticking out over her ear. An ornate veil covered her eyes. My grandfather was dressed in an elegant pin-striped suit and a dark tie. He stood tall, smoking a cigar.

I was continually trying to engage her.

"Let me show you Rachel's new fiancé, Ma."

"Here are the pictures from my wedding, Ma. Remember that dress you wore?"

As the family expanded, each new grandchild generated endless photos: first smile, first steps, first birthday party, first day of school. Eventually the box was overflowing with reminders of the life my mother had lived, the family she'd raised, the people she'd loved dearly and who'd loved her back.

In early 2004, my mother's neurologist told us that her PD had progressed. Based on talking with her, he believed she had Lewy body dementia, which often develops after many years of Parkinson's. I had no idea what that meant until the end of the year.

A short time after that appointment, I arrived at my mother's apartment. It was a bitter December afternoon, two days after what would have been my father's birthday, December 24, 2004. We had buried him more than three decades before, but his birthday was a date I always approached with sadness. Perhaps, too, my new worries about my mother were accentuating Dad's death. "You would have been ninety-three years old now," I whispered to the fifty-four-year-old father I buried.

When I opened the door to my mother's apartment, I shouldn't have been surprised to see her sitting before the television, her constant companion. Although I couldn't tell whether she was watching, it was replaying the same horrifying footage I'd been seeing all morning at home: the devastation unleashed by the Indian Ocean tsunami. Within a day or two, 228,000 people in fourteen countries would be swept away.

One particularly horrific scene of destruction had caught the attention of the reporter: the popular tourist destination of Phuket, Thailand. Rachel and I had spent an amazing week on this serene beach one winter in the early '80s when she was between high school and college. As I walked into my mother's room, I was once again stunned by the tsunami's destruction. Gale-force winds and rushing waters were toppling hotels, crumbling bungalows, and washing human beings out to sea. When I burst into tears, my mother, who had been staring into space, asked me what was wrong.

"Take a look, Ma—I've been watching this all morning!" I said tearfully.

Although she was gazing at the television screen, she was unmoved. "What's going on?" she asked innocently.

For a moment, I could not speak. At first I was startled;

then, perhaps I was overwhelmed with grief. She had slipped into a new arena.

"Ma," I said, "look at all those people—swept away, gone!"

My mother continued watching silently, blankly. Her cognitive functioning was not what I'd thought it to be. I took a deep breath.

Another layer of loss.

Dinner at the

Manhattan Grille, 2005

Larry and I had been married for almost a decade, and by now my mother had been living with Parkinson's for four years. Now she moved slowly, struggling with stiffness from muscle rigidity. Lewy body dementia had left her more lethargic and with more severe memory swings. Holding a fork challenged her, as did carrying on a conversation for more than a few minutes. Her functioning was unpredictable. She swung from good to bad moments, from good to bad days, but she was declining steadily. She had aides twenty-four hours per day. Luckily, she lived nearby, so I could visit her two or three times every week. Being with her was frustrating and heartbreaking. Often I felt worn out after only a few minutes, and I had come to the decision that these short visits each week were the best I could do.

It was a Sunday night, and Larry and I were taking my mother out to dinner. Both the meal and our conversation dragged on in a predictable, painfully slow, and repetitive manner.

"How's Zach?" my mother asked.

I filled her in on details about my son's new baby.

"And Rachel?"

I told her about Rachel's new job.

"And how's Zach?"

My stomach dropped. I was weary of trying to figure out how to handle this. *If I tell her she's repeating herself, will I make her feel ashamed or humiliated? Or won't my comment register? If I answer the question again, will she simply ask it yet another time?*

"Zach's fine, Ma, really fine."

"How's your mother doing?" I asked Larry. Maybe discussing his mother's recent hospitalization would interest my mom. Larry gave us an update on his mother's recent gallbladder surgery, but I couldn't really tell what my mother took in. My heart began to race. I had held the belief that my mother derived some modicum of comfort from just being in our presence, hearing our familiar voices, but this dinner conversation was sorely challenging that idea.

Finally, the bill arrived.

"Another cup of tea for me, please. Is there time?" she asked politely, pathetically. I understood that although my mother was no longer totally here, neither was she gone. She was astute enough to know that the arrival of a bill meant this meal would soon be over, enough to know that sitting together in a restaurant with her daughter and son-in-law was far better than being at home in bed, with only the company of her television. I understood that she didn't want this moment to end. Our companionship mattered, and that was why we were here.

The sour look on Larry's face said it all; he was bored and exasperated. He was eager to take my mother home, get in a cab, and be done with this trying meal.

"Peggy, you can't imagine what I have to do before Monday morning! My desk is piled high!" he said. He began itemizing all the work he had to finish up: papers to read, emails to return. Of course, she didn't follow the details, but I saw her face fall.

"If you need to go, Larry, I'll meet you at home," I said calmly, masking my feelings of irritation and disappointment. I understood why Larry wanted to leave, but what I wished was that he would stay with me. Balancing our needs was never easy nor had it been with any of my previous partners. By now, I knew that my mother was correct about one thing: Marriage *is* difficult.

My benign response was all the permission my husband needed to begin packing up. He apologized to my mother, told us again about the endless work awaiting him at home, gave us each a peck on the cheek, and put on his coat, and then—poof—he was gone.

Sitting at our favorite window table, my mother and I watched him hail a taxi. Then my mother turned to me and said, "You're upset at him. Just let it go."

I was amazed. Her mental states fluctuated wildly, but I saw that at this moment she was with it. She had followed the subtleties of our interaction and picked up on my annoyance and frustration with my husband.

"I *am* upset, Ma. I'm not like you. I can't just let important things go," I said.

"Don't let him upset you," she said. "It's not worth it. We had a perfectly nice dinner together."

"But, Ma," I said, "it *does* upset me when my husband is rude and self-centered. There's no reason he had to rush out of here!"

"Don't aggravate yourself," she said. "He's not going to change."

I knew enough about my mother's long-standing perspective on men being difficult and people in general being unable or unlikely to change. By now, I also knew the ups and downs of her Parkinson's enough to avoid a challenging conversation with her, but she interrupted my thoughts.

"Just remember what I've told you, more than once before: Let it go. Don't get divorced again. Just..." She didn't finish the sentence. She didn't have to.

I reached across the table and took her small, gnarled hands in mine. As I wrapped my fingers around hers, I noticed the sun spots. I felt her frailty. I leaned across the table and gave her a hug. "Don't worry, Ma," I said. "Mother knows best."

We both laughed.

PART SEVEN:

Waiting

Imagine that your mother is standing in the doorway of a room you are seated in. See her searching. She is looking for you, and when she finds you, she wants to come in and sit by you. How do you feel in your body as your mother spots you? Have you made eye contact? If so, what's that like? Check in with yourself. Do you look at her with a welcoming gaze, or do you turn away? How do you feel about her coming into the room and sitting beside you?

Come Now

The dingy church basement was alive with the buzz of *djembes*, *doumbeks*, and tambourines. Setting up my drum, I suddenly noticed my phone vibrating. I considered not answering. The sounds were deafening—this was no place for a phone conversation—and I was eager to unpack and get into the drum circle. Thursday night practice with my women's drumming group, the Druumatics, was now the highlight of my week. I'd been coming out to Long Island to take lessons for the past year, and now I'd been invited to join them in what would be my first performance.

My phone continued to vibrate. I hated being an electronic prisoner, but I slipped my hand into my pocket to take a peek. The area code of the number that popped up grabbed me—could it be my mother's hospice? I scurried out of the drum circle, stepped into the hallway, and breathlessly flipped open my phone.

"Good evening, Judy. It's Jake from Zicklin."

I stopped breathing. If the director of the Zicklin hospice was calling me himself, it must be serious. I ducked into a small, stuffy alcove. My hands were clammy; I hoped I wouldn't drop the phone.

"I think the end is near now, Judy," Jake said. "Come."

215

His directness stunned me. *How can he be so certain? Don't I need time to prepare?* "Now?" I asked.

"Now. Or as soon as you can."

My heart started to race, and I was sweating. I felt like I was suffocating.

"An hour earlier, your mother began retching. You know she hasn't been eating much, right?" Jake paused, as if to give me a moment to process his news. I'd visited my mother the night before and knew she'd eaten only a cracker or two in the prior twenty-four hours. The only liquid she'd absorbed was from ice chips that Penny, her aide, had given her.

"Since she has so little food in her," he continued, "compulsive vomiting is probably a sign the body is giving up. We can never say for sure when someone will go, Judy, but I believe she's on her way."

I heard Jake hang up. I was standing in the hallway, holding my cell phone. In the background, the drumbeats throbbed. The drummers were working on our opening performance number, "Coo-Coo," following our leader, Sharon, who was barking out rapid-fire instructions. Her voice was strong and deep.

"Let's get it right this time, girls! Five, six, seven, eight; tone, tone, slap, slap." It was the pattern I had been practicing at home. "Let it breathe," she instructed, reminding the group to slow down the pace between the musical phrases. I was lost, swinging wildly between the pounding of the drums and that of my heavy heart.

Jake's call should have been no surprise—I had been both dreading and anticipating this moment—but I was in shock. My ninety-three-year-old mother was a hospice patient with a terminal diagnosis. She was wheelchair bound and had been slipping away, mentally and physically, suffering from Parkinson's and dementia for years. She had been in hospice for two months, and her decline had been radical. But even though she had been barely eating, hardly moving, rarely talking, and sleeping twenty hours per day, I was not ready to hear that she might be leaving this earth, tonight, even though part of me yearned to let her go and get on with my own life.

Still sitting in the alcove of the practice room, I was jolted back to reality. Jake had said, "Come now!" but I hadn't moved.

I picked up my phone again and called Larry. When he answered, I could not speak. "It's me, Judy," I finally said.

"I know it's you, hon, I can barely hear you. What's up?"

"I got a call from Jake at Zicklin. It's my mother." I could barely get out the next sentence. "Jake said to come now." The steady drumbeat in the background made it hard for me to focus as I repeated my conversation with Jake.

"Oh, no," Larry said. Hearing the tenderness in his voice made me tear up. I took a deep breath but still could not speak.

"Jude, I'm so sorry. Come back to New York, now, and we'll go up to your mother together," Larry said. "Honey, you gotta leave now. Pack up your drum; don't forget anything." His calm voice and slow directions centered me.

I told him I would leave, but the words were barely out of my mouth before I began to sob. How would I go back into the practice room? What would I say? The thought of telling my drummer friends that my mother was dying made me gasp for air. I couldn't say those words.

"Calm down, honey," Larry said. "Go back into the practice session and tell them you have to leave; it's an emergency. Don't drive to the city. Leave your car at the train station and take the next train."

I was woozy, but I knew he was giving me good advice. I asked him to throw my toothbrush and a bathrobe into a shopping bag in case I wound up sleeping at the hospice.

When I returned to the practice session, the music was deafening, jarring. Everyone was playing and swaying, and a few women were dancing to the rhythm of the jangling bells piercing the air. I was barely noticed as I began packing up my drum, but suddenly, the room was still.

"What's wrong, Judy? Where are you going?" asked Adrienne, the oldest woman in our group, who was sitting next to me. Unable to speak, I dropped into my chair. Adrienne cradled my trembling shoulders.

Pulling out of the parking lot, I started making calls. Neither my brother nor my son was reachable. Miraculously, Rachel, who has a reputation for never answering the phone, picked up. Just the sound of her voice triggered my tears. I could not stop crying.

Half an hour later, I was on an almost deserted train to New York. I could still hear the rhythm of the drums pounding in my head. I had no way of knowing that the days of the drum group were numbered and that within the year, Hurricane Sandy would flood the entire south shore of Long Island, including the one-hundred-year-old church where our practice sessions took place.

I was seated in the back of a yellow cab, traveling up Eighth Avenue, when Larry called. "Just checking in on you," he said gently.

"On my way," I told him. It had been more than two hours since Jake called, and my mother might already be gone. This shouldn't have surprised me. It had been just the previous night—twenty-four hours earlier—that I'd visited her, and when I left, I had feared the worst.

The Last Visit

That night, I had just finished meeting with my Wednesday night therapy group and was getting ready for my weekly trip to Long Island, when I realized I hadn't seen my mother for a few days. Now that she was living in a hospice in Riverdale, visiting her was no longer as convenient as it had been when she'd been around the corner from me, in assisted living on West Eighty-Sixth Street.

As I was packing up, Larry walked into the bedroom. "You're going to Riverdale? Now? It's cold and drizzly tonight. Foggy, too. The roads will be slick."

The weather was bad, and ever since my fiancé Michael had died, I'd avoided driving on slippery roads whenever I could.

"And besides, Judy," Larry added, "Your mother probably won't even know if you come or not."

Of course, part of me could see his point of view—what was the point of visiting if she wouldn't even remember I was there? Just the week before, my mom had asked me how my brother, John, was doing; I don't remember what I said, but I remember how pained I felt when I realized she had no recollection that he'd visited her the day before. But I was committed to another path. The time we spent together mattered to me, and, I hoped, to her. Anyway, Larry tended to worry, and sometimes I ignored his apprehensions. Most important, a nagging voice within me, a good-daughter voice, was relentlessly reminding me how empty and lonely and scared my mother must be.

———————

When the elevator opened at her floor, I held on to the wall railing to brace myself. *Get prepared; take a deep breath*, I reminded myself each time I arrived.

It was never easy to take in the eerie silence: twenty-five rooms, all the doors closed, and barely a sound in the hallway. You'd think the place was vacant. With silent patients and a respectful, quiet staff, there was practically no noise, unlike my other experiences in hospitals or rehabs, filled with busy, often too-cheery nurses and aides. Here, there was no chit-chat, not even much normal conversation. This was the serious business of dying. It felt like a stage set preparing me for the great beyond. A quick left to her room, and I paused. I never knew if she would be awake.

When I opened the door, I was surprised that my mother was not in bed, where I usually found her. She was sitting up in the one lounge chair in the room, brightly lit by the standing lamp behind her chair. She looked a bit unbalanced, as if Penny, her aide, had propped her up.

Penny was a large, black woman from Jamaica. She had been caring for my mother for the past seven years and had been much more than an aide; she had been a friend, a sister, a loving eyewitness, an angel—with us for these long years of deterioration. I was always surprised how attuned Penny was with not only to my mother but to me and how tender she was when she gave me bad news. She was wearing her signature black wool hat, which softly framed her gentle face, and a wooly cardigan sweater, even though the room was warm. Her big brown eyes were full but fearless.

"She's not doing so well today," Penny said.

Again, just as I did each time I saw her, I had to readjust to the fact that my once meticulously groomed mother was gone. In her place sat a tired, washed-out version of her former self, a woman whose face was marbled with deep wrinkles. No longer dressed in cashmere and silk, my mother was disheveled, disoriented, slumped over, eyes closed, wearing a faded and stained navy warm-up suit. Her gray hair was thin, wild, and unkempt, her skin blotchy, and she had a scab near her left eye. I hardly recognized her.

"Hi, Mom, it's me, Judy. I'm going out to Long Island. Larry and I are spending the weekend there. I wanted to stop over to say hello before I left the city."

Her eyes remained closed.

"I'll see my Thursday patients I still have out there, and then I have drum-group practice tomorrow night."

No response. Having nothing new to say, I stumbled but continued, a bit more loudly. "Do you remember when my drum group came to the Atria, Ma, when you were living around the corner from me on the Upper West Side?"

At the mention of the drum group, my mom's eyes opened. A few years back, I'd brought my drum teacher to give me lessons in her apartment in the Atria, hoping to give my mother something novel to look forward to. Unfortunately, she had hated the noise.

She peeked out at me but, after a slow yawn, sighed and quickly closed her eyes again.

"Tomorrow I have six hours of sessions in my Long Island office, Ma. Then it's on to drum practice."

She remained silent, and I felt exhausted. I was aware that making conversation with her had always required me to stretch. I had never been sure about our contact; I felt that now more than ever.

"I have some new pictures for you." I placed a photograph in her frail hands, noticing her pronounced purplish veins, which actually scared me. I hoped they would not be part of my genetic inheritance.

"This is Rachel with her baby, Jett."

My mother looked blank. I kept forgetting how Parkinson's had ravaged her mind.

"Rachel, Ma. I'm talking about my daughter, your granddaughter."

It occurred to me that if my mother had been her old self, she would have balked at his name. "Jett?" she'd say, "Rachel named her baby Jett? Where do they get these new names? Where did she get the name Jett? Isn't that the name of a plane?" But as quickly as the thought drifted in, I let it go. It was upsetting how often I had to remind myself that we were in a new phase. Those glib remarks were over. Now I wasn't even sure if she remembered who Rachel was.

"Mom! Jett is six months old now. He's your eighth great-grandchild. Did you ever think you'd have so many great-grandchildren? And I'm blessed with three grandsons!" The enthusiasm I had to muster in my attempt to relate to my unreachable mother evoked a lifelong ache, my yearning to connect deeply.

The picture of Jett I placed in her hand fluttered down to the floor. Clearly, my mom didn't realize it. In the millisecond between when Penny picked it up and when she started to replace it in my mother's hand, I recalled a visit from my mother when I was a young mom.

Rachel was three months old, and my mother arrived with a gift, a pale gray snowsuit decorated with small orange elephants.

"Can we try it on her now? I have to see how cute she looks in it!" my mother said, unwrapping the box. It was adorable, and I was particularly pleased that my mother had paid attention to my new feminist aversion to the color pink.

"Let's have a mother-daughter fashion show," she suggested, as she pulled out another box: a gift for me. Somehow she'd found a match: a gray T-shirt with orange elephants. How much positive energy she exuded back then, always bustling in with a box of pastries or a coloring book or a surprise of some sort. Just recalling her bounce and generosity—who she was then compared with who she was now, in hospice— left me feeling sad for both of us.

While I was lost in thought, Penny had picked up the photo and gently put it back in my mother's hands. Within moments, it again drifted downward, landing by her chair. What surprised me was how stirred up I was. I knew my mother was no longer able to maintain a connection, but my mind went to a dark place. How many times had I felt dropped by my mother, who could never offer me the deep knowing I yearned for so badly?

Penny and I locked eyes, and I shook my head. *No point in picking it up and replacing it,* I hoped to communicate.

"Good night, Mom. Gotta go. I'll see you after the weekend." Our visit was only half an hour, but I was spent, between trying to make conversation and listening to Penny detailing my mom's daily existence. There was a time when leaving my mother was painful, when she was begging me to stay a bit longer whenever I mentioned leaving, but that time was long gone.

Driving out to Long Island, I found myself wondering if my mom was still sitting in the black leather recliner, eyes glazed over or closed, dozing. Maybe Penny had helped her into her nightgown. Maybe Larry was right—maybe my mother hadn't really taken me in—or my visit. I felt a big sigh escape. *How many more years will this go on? How long will I be schlepping back and forth to Riverdale, caring and worrying and resenting while managing the endless details of my mother's life?*

When the taxi from the train station pulled up to our building, Larry was standing outside. Taking in the sight of him—tall, with salt-and-pepper hair—I felt his loving embrace even before he opened the cab door.

"Hi, babe," he said, climbing in and pulling me close to him, wrapping his arms around me. The warmth from his bear hug comforted me instantly. I melted into him, sank into his chest, and breathed in the familiar aroma of his aftershave.

"There's nothing new to tell you," I said, and he interrupted me with a kiss.

"Don't say anything," he said, pulling me closer. "Just close your eyes and be with me."

Traffic crawled.

Forty minutes later, we reached Zicklin.

When we got off the elevator and arrived at my mother's room, Penny was standing at the door, waiting to greet us. I rushed over to my mother's bedside and found her under the covers, eyes closed. She looked so pale and tiny, it scared me. Penny had followed me, and when I turned, I found her standing a few feet away. Her big brown eyes seemed wider than usual. She hugged me tightly, and I sank into her warm, soft body.

"Things are not good, Judy," she said, slowly and softly. She glanced over at my mother, who was lying very still, and then looked back at me. "She's been like this for hours."

She hugged me again and held onto me, and for a moment I wasn't sure who was holding up whom. "I waited till you came," Penny said. She didn't say what was obvious—her workday was long over, but she didn't want my mother to die alone. Now that we were here, she could leave.

Putting on her coat and scarf, Penny took her time bundling up. In Jamaica, it's rarely below seventy-five degrees, and she often talked about how cold it was in New York, but tonight, she said nothing. Finally dressed, she stood at the door. Hand on the doorknob, she locked eyes with me. "I will see you tomorrow, Judy," she said. There was no need to say what we both knew. My mother might be gone by morning.

"I'll call you if anything happens," I said, taking refuge in the euphemism.

Instead of leaving, Penny turned and walked across the room, back over to my mother's bedside. She bent over and kissed my mother gently on the forehead.

"Good night, my dear Peggy," she whispered. "This may be goodbye, too. Pleasant dreams."

Before she left, I hugged her again, hard.

———————

My husband and I were settled into the two chairs we had placed by my mother's bedside, when Arlene, one of the hospice nurses, arrived. Softly, she reminded me that even though my mother was not moving, just lying still, breathing ever so lightly, she was alive.

"The dying are alive," she said. "The dying are living. Our dying need to be reassured we will be okay without them."

I was touched by how she spoke about "our" dying. Too many in the hospice were facing death alone.

I'd heard this message before, at other deaths, earlier losses—the dying are alive—but this time was different. This time, it was my mother who was dying. *My* mother.

We had dimmed the lights in her room, which was sparsely furnished, with just the hospital bed, two chairs, and a dresser. Many hospice residents are barely aware of their surroundings, I was told when we moved her in. Even so, I couldn't resist bringing some of her personal possessions over: an antique vase she loved and a few family photos. The moon streamed in and illuminated one of the photographs on top of the dresser: a snapshot of my brother and me at a Paul Simon concert in East Hampton in the early '90s. John, who was now graying, in the photo had a full head of thick, long brown hair, and I was wearing a purple tie-dyed dress. My hair was long and braided. How young and exuberant we were!

I moved my chair closer to my mother's bed and held her hand. Her face was masklike. Her hand felt so small, so light, and so hot. I couldn't understand why or how she was so hot. No one had ever told me about heat at the end. I touched her face and her arm. Hot, too. Her head was on a pillow, her eyes closed.

"It takes a lot of work to die," Arlene reminded me before she slipped out the door.

"Ma," I said, holding her hot hand, "your time may be near. It may be here." Her eyes remained shut, and she did not move. My throat was constricted. I was afraid it would close. I wondered if my mother could hear me. My head pounded. "Ma, I will sit here with you and hold your hand. Your time is coming, and if you want to let go . . . when you have to let go . . . I will be here." Larry was sitting to my right, and each time I spoke, he squeezed my hand, reminding me I was not alone, that he was at my side, literally and figuratively.

My mother didn't blink or move or respond. All I could hear was my own breathing. *In and out*, I reminded myself. *Try to be calm; just inhale, exhale, and let go.*

In these eleven years of Parkinson's and dementia, we had had other close calls, but this time felt different. There had been other times when I'd told her, "Mom, when it's your time, I'll be with you," but I realized this time was not the same. "When" had come. "When" was now.

"Ma," I said, "I will hold your hand like you have held mine."

At that moment, a buzz from my cell phone interrupted me. I let go of Larry's hand, flipped open my phone. It was a call from Marni, a patient. She had left my office the night before in tears. I didn't take the call, but I had switched gears. I closed the phone and my eyes.

Twenty-four hours ago, I was in my office. Now, I'm on my mother's death watch.

Twenty-four hours ago, my patient Marni was crying, feeling inadequate after being upstaged by the "belle of the ball," her still beautiful, eighty-four-year-old mother.

One of my mother's favorite expressions, "belle of the ball," had echoed after Marni left my office. I could hear my mother's voice and see her eyes flash as she told a story about her and her best friend, Natalie.

"We were showstoppers!" she would say proudly. I'd heard the story many times but always appreciated the joy my mother experienced in telling this tale. At sixteen, they'd gone to a fancy party and intentionally arrived late in twin, drop-dead-gorgeous black velvet dresses.

"Making a late entry always pays off," my mother would say. I smiled thinking about her. She had had her day!

The Pink Cashmere
Sweater Set

I was twelve years old. It was the day before my friend Hilda's party, which would be a boy-girl party. I was nervous about what to wear—I was supposed to get "dressed up," but what did that really mean?

My mother sat on my bed, smiling calmly while I tried on and discarded skirts, blouses, and dresses. The pile of rejects on the floor beside me grew.

My mom always looks so beautiful. Her long hair is swept up on her head, just like Betty Grable's, her favorite movie star. How did she ever learn to put up her hair in that elaborate twist? And where did she find that ribbon for her hair, a perfect match for the light blue sweater set she's wearing?

Suddenly, she jumped off my bed and grabbed my hand. "Your navy skirt will be perfect," she said, as she gleefully opened my closet door, swept through the hangers on the clothes rack, and pulled out the skirt.

"Try it on, dear," she said, squeezing my hand.

I eagerly slipped the skirt on over my head, pulling it down and straightening the seams.

My mom was right. The skirt fit perfectly, hugging and flowing where it should. She was so smart, my mom!

"What will I wear it with?" I asked.

She frowned, and I saw how hard she was thinking. Then, a smile overtook her face and her eyes twinkled. "What about my new pink cashmere sweater set? It will be fabulous with this skirt, dear!"

I could not speak. *My mother is offering to loan me her brand-new, very soft, and very expensive pale pink cashmere sweater set!* I'd had my eye on it since the moment she swooped it off the shelf in May's department store that rainy day in May. I had spied it on a sale table. The red-and-black sign caught my eye: END-OF-SEASON SALE: $39 FOR TWO PIECES.

Thirty-nine dollars, even for the two pieces together, was a lot of money for my family in those days.

"Really, Ma, really?" I finally got the words out. She has worn the sweater set only once or twice, and now she was offering to loan it to me?

"Really." She nodded, rushing out of the room to get it.

Alone, I gazed at myself in the mirror. My baggy under-shirt bra looked so awkward hanging loosely from my bony chest. My mom had tried to reassure me that bosoms were in my future, but I was neither comforted nor convinced.

Moments later, she reappeared, carrying one of her special, airtight plastic bags in her arms. Sealed inside was the pale pink sweater set, carefully folded.

"Try it on—it goes so beautifully with your complexion, and with the skirt."

What is she talking about? My complexion? Is she referring to my freckles? Or my zits?

She unzipped the plastic bag and placed the sweater set in my hands.

I carefully slipped into it—first the pullover, then the cardigan. So soft. So elegant. So sexy. Me?

"Perfect, dear." She beamed.

The night of the party, she applauded when I stepped into the kitchen.

"Take these," she said, as she clasped a strand of pearls around my neck.

Within moments, we were in our blue Chevy convertible, off to the party. At Hilda's house, she stopped, leaned over, and gave me a peck on the cheek.

"I'll be back for you at eleven o'clock," she said, reminding me of my curfew. She squeezed my hand as she said, "You are going to wow everyone—you're going to be the belle of the ball!"

The front door of Hilda's house was open. Standing in the doorway, I could see boys on the left, girls on the right. Hilda's living room was crowded with kids I knew, as well as some unfamiliar faces. I spotted Patsy and Kathy, both wearing the shirtwaist dresses they wore to school; maybe I was too dressed up? I slipped into the huge room and inched my way over to the girls' side. Within moments, I was huddled deep in the throng of giggling females. Daringly, we eyed the other side: the boys. Johnny Mathis's voice floated from the Victrola, filling the house as he crooned "Chances Are," low and silky. I scanned the room furtively. *What are my chances? Is there a boy with a silly grin here, waiting for me?*

First music; then dancing.

"May I have this dance?"

"May I have the next dance?"

"It's my turn now!"

The boys had lined up! Peter, the kid with the wavy hair; Rich (oh no!), oozing pimples galore; Tommy, the fastest runner in our grade—my dad said he was heading for the Olympics. They were swarming, jostling each other out of the way to be next in line for a dance with me. My mom's words echoed: "belle of the ball." I couldn't believe I was being noticed like this. Me? I had thought nobody would even look at me.

Suddenly, a boy with a silly grin caught my eye.

It's Billy—he lives around the corner and has a shiny new three-speed bike with skinny tires. How cool! I pray my sweat is invisible. He's walking across the room . . . coming over to me. He's smiling . . . and looking straight at me. I can't breathe.

Within moments, I felt a hand on my shoulder. The heat from his sweaty palm penetrated the soft cashmere, and I trembled with excitement and fear. But my words slipped out of my mouth, unplanned, effortlessly, gracefully, and I heard myself say, "Yes, yes, of course, I'd love to dance with you."

We were out on the dance floor. The Victrola was belting out a slow Frank Sinatra song, and we were doing the box step. Although Billy was holding me at arms' length, he felt a little too close. I heard my mom's voice and had the courage to gently move away while smiling at him. Thankfully, a fast song replaced the slow Sinatra number, and the next thing I knew, Billy was twirling me around the room and I was hanging on to him tightly. Out of the corner of my eye, I could see his silly grin. My heart was pounding so loudly, I wondered if he could hear it.

I glanced around and saw the pack of girls watching me floating in another galaxy with Billy. *How did he choose me?* I wondered. In my twelve-year-old brain, there was only one possible reason—my mother's pink cashmere sweater set was what set me apart. It was my mother who had helped me become the belle of the ball.

Sitting in my office after my session with Marni, I was amazed at the curious workings of my mind. Now, as I was losing my mother, I was seeing more of her gifts than ever before. Listening to Marni's story about how her mother's maternal narcissism damaged her had evoked my awareness of how my own mother promoted and enjoyed nourishing my own healthy narcissism. In loaning me her new pink sweater set, she gave me something far more precious than the soft cashmere. She passed the torch. It was as if she knew how it was to be the object of longing and was handing down her secrets to me. She gave me her vote of confidence, along with a legacy gift—the belief that I could and should wear the belle-of-the-ball mantle.

As my eyes filled, I noticed a sense of fullness and warmth spreading through my body. Tears of joy were bubbling up. I recalled the question I asked patients when I saw positive emotions, such as pleasure and joy, arise: "Is there more?" Often we therapists are more comfortable digging for pain than highlighting joy and pleasure, more at home with darkness than with light. While owning and mourning our sorrows is always part of growth and healing, achieving wholeness means being able to seize our inner light.

"Is there more?" I asked myself, and my "yes" tumbled out. My mother gave me not only the twinkle in her eye and her broad, inviting smile but also those threads of cashmere—rich, nourishing soil that empowered me to cultivate desire, excitement, and pride. Woven into those threads were the roots of confidence. Woven into those threads were the seeds of permission—permission to be comfortable and find pleasure in my body and my sexuality.

The Jane Brody Ritual

I had never imagined my mother would develop a degenerative disease like Parkinson's. But in the many years of her slow decline, I learned a lot about myself. I learned how impatient I was, and I was forced to practice strengthening my "patience" muscle. I learned how to speak slowly. I learned how to offer small bits of information. I got used to repeating myself. I learned how to create a semblance of normalcy in a totally unexpected, unreal situation.

Early on, back when my mother was still able to live independently in her home, I stumbled upon a solution: reading aloud to her. Jane Brody being her favorite columnist, "Well" columns from the *New York Times* were my first choice. Reading aloud enlivened me; any of Jane's topics—healthy eating, osteoporosis, bullying, recovering from alcoholism, widowhood, or postpartum depression—was interesting and far better than trying to make tedious conversation. Eventually, I began bringing Chinese food for lunch, and I'd read aloud while we ate.

"I used to be the one doing the reading to you," my mother once announced.

I was surprised to hear her comment about our obvious role reversal.

"I remember when you had never even heard of Jane Brody!" she said. She loved to recall her own zest during the era when I was exhausted, busy getting my PhD while raising two small children.

"I remember when I never read an entire newspaper," I told her. "I could barely get past the headlines and what I picked up on the radio while carpooling the kids around. You were my personal newscaster, Mom, quoting columnists I had never heard of and sending me erudite editorials in the mail."

Later on, when I recalled a book she had read to me when I was a child, *The Little Engine That Could*, she didn't remember it. A week or two later, I arrived with the book.

"Does it look familiar?" I asked. It didn't. "I'll read a few pages aloud." When I looked over at her, I could tell she wasn't following the story.

But back in those early days of our Tuesday ritual, she loved reminiscing. She was especially proud that after the death of her second husband, she'd gone to college. "A bachelor's degree from Fordham University at sixty-three! Not bad!" she'd say. She was right.

As time passed, even after her mind had begun to slip and she no longer could follow the stories, I read her the Jane Brody columns. They not only kept me awake but also did much more. This ritual connected us, one to another, and my mother to her past life. It allowed us to keep up the pretense that we were sharing ideas, while in fact what we were really sharing was a new way of simply being together.

As her memory slipped, I switched gears again. Often, I read passages aloud from novels I knew she'd enjoyed when she was younger. I started with *Gone With the Wind*. We had watched the movie together so many times over the years I was certain the story would be familiar.

"Her name is Scarlett? I didn't remember that," she admitted.

Once, I boldly read her a bad-mommy story I'd written about me as an unhappy ten-year-old. I'd been at sleepaway camp for eight miserable weeks, longing to come home. Finally, the summer was over. How eager I was to see her. But when our camp train arrived at Grand Central Station, no Mommy. She was an hour late to pick me up. Waiting and worrying, I was petrified I'd be there forever, forgotten and swallowed up in the bowels of the mammoth, underground train station.

"Did that really happen?" she asked.

"It did, Ma. Don't you remember?"

She shook her head. She didn't.

"Can you imagine how scared I was, Ma?"

"I don't know what you're talking about," she said, "but, you know, my memory really isn't good anymore. But even if it happened, you turned out just fine, right?"

I shrugged. *Just fine? Just fine?* There was that phrase I hated. I'd heard it all my life. I heard it when my best friend dumped me. I heard it when I was homesick at sleepaway camp, I heard it later on, when my fiancé was killed in a car accident. Eventually, I got used to knowing that whenever I talked about something upsetting, she would brush my words away and dismiss my feelings with her predictable response, "You'll be fine, honey."

Sometimes the phrase felt like innocuous filler. Other times, it seemed to be shorthand for "why complain?" This enraged me.

"Why not complain when there's something to complain about, Ma?" I said, challenging her when I got older. I'd spent years telling one of my early therapists how impossible it was to connect with my Pollyanna-ish mother, so unlike me. I seemed to have been born with a propensity to gravitate to dark places, while my mother, allergic to complaining about anything, was wired to minimize pain and suffering, her own and mine.

She had a slew of remarks all meant to drive home her quintessential practical, optimistic message, for example, "Into each life some rain will fall." Her remedy? According to her, we must "grin and bear" our troubles. "People don't like to hear your problems" was another of her deep-seated beliefs, which undoubtedly fueled my inspiration to become a psychologist. I actually wanted to listen to people discuss their problems and help them learn how to resolve them.

Inhale Deeply,

Exhale Completely

Friday, 10:00 a.m., day two of the vigil. I had been sitting by my mother's bedside for not even an hour, and I was already worn out. My mind soared, zoomed, settled, stagnated. Every once in a while, I heard my mother gasp or saw her move and my heart started to race, until I realized it was only my imagination. I felt like I was in a trance. I sat, daydreamed, checked my phone, worried, wandered, remembered. My mother didn't blink, didn't move. Her face was immobile. Her body was now a slight lump resting beneath sheets tucked in with hospital corners that reminded me of how I was taught to make my bed at camp.

Ten years old when I first went to sleepaway camp, I was miserably homesick. I hated the counselors; the freezing-cold New Hampshire lake, full of slimy leeches; and the hospital corners, the gold standard for evaluation. Being a good camper, bunkmate, and team player was the ethos, even though for most of the summer I had a pain in my stomach. I missed my mom.

I remember a conversation with my mother when Rachel, at eight, wanted to follow in her older brother's footsteps and go to sleepaway camp.

"Judy, you will have the best summer with both kids gone!" my mother said.

"Ma, I don't think Rachel is old enough."

"Judy, you worry too much. She's a grown-up eight."

"Don't you remember how homesick I was, Ma? I cried every day!"

"You were fine! You were captain of the softball team!"

"I wasn't fine! I wasn't ready to go to camp then, Ma."

Sitting by my mother's bedside, I drifted through time, backward and forward. When my father died, we didn't have cell phones to keep us company as we sat for long hours. Now, I was comforted as I listened to messages from Rachel and Zach, both thousands of miles away.

"When should we come, Ma?" my daughter asked.

"How are you doing, Mom?" my son asked.

Emails and texts sustained me, reminded me that my children were with me in spirit, but I had nothing new to say to them or to anyone. When would this waiting come to an end? My heart was racing. I was filled with both dread and longing.

I fast-forwarded time. How long would it be until I was lying in a bed with hospital corners while my son and daughter sat by my side? When my mother was gone, I would be on the front line, and from all my reading, I knew that taking care of her had pushed me into thinking about and accepting my own aging, something I'd been able to avoid until now. I had no way of knowing that only three years after my mother died, my son would sit by my side as I recovered from a mastectomy. As my recovery moved along, I would lie on the couch when my daughter visited, too scared and too weak to play with my grandchildren. What would stun me was how much I missed my mother.

Inhale deeply, exhale completely, and let whatever happens, happen. As I inhaled and exhaled, just hearing the hum of the very same words I said to help my patients, I calmed down. Somewhere between my breathing in and out, Larry arrived. He stepped out into the hallway to talk to Arlene, the hospice nurse, and while I couldn't detect the words, the sound of his voice warmed me as I sat, watching my mother. *Nothing to do, nowhere to go—just breathe.* How many times had I said these words, hoping to bring quiet and comfort to a distraught patient in my office, and now here I was, talking to myself, my own words echoing and soothing me. I looked around the small, bare room, the room my mother would die in. By now, I was familiar with every crack in the ceiling, every crease in the drapes, the whirring sound of the heating apparatus turning on and off, the buzz of the machines clicking, monitoring my mother's vitals.

I tried to read, but concentrating was impossible. My thoughts wandered. My eyes landed on the large picture window across from me. I stared into the black night outside. Outside was a million miles away. The world whirred on while I was here, stuck inside counting cracks and creases. *Deep breaths.*

Two o'clock. Three o'clock. Four o'clock. I had been at the hospice all day. I kept expecting my mother to move or speak, but no, she was doing neither, and barely breathing. Soon it would be twenty-four hours of her being like this. Every hour was a message: *The end is near. The end is here.*

"Mom, I know we're at the end," I said. "You have done your job, and done it well. You have given me enough."

As I uttered these words, holding her hot hand tightly, I realized what I was saying was true. My own children had teased me, referring to my love as unconditional, "like cement." Nothing they had ever done or said had altered my deep connection to them—no hurt, no disappointment could sever my love for them. Although for much of my life I mourned that my mother was not all I needed, I knew that she had been there for me. I knew that my ability to mother my own children was connected to the mothering I received, for better or for worse. If I had given my children unconditional love, maybe I had received something permanent and stabilizing and life-affirming from her.

My mind was perpetually spinning. One minute I was steady; the next, I was filled with dark questions. What if my mother had been different? Given me more? What if she had always made me feel safe and understood? Would I have been better off? Perhaps I never would have searched for a deeper connection with my husband. Perhaps I never would have gone in search of my own psychotherapy. Perhaps I never would have become a therapist.

"Mom, I want to tell you something: I have enough. You gave me enough to have enough. I have a great husband who loves me, and I have Zach and Rachel and their adorable children. You know how close I am to Zach's Rebecca and Rachel's Miki—how lucky am I that my children married people whom I love and who love me. I am blessed, Ma, with three precious grandsons: Sammy, Nat, and Jett."

Just saying these words, I sank into a bittersweet sadness and appreciation for all she built and for what was missing, too, for what we now shared and for what I was about to lose. Her eyes were closed, her face was immobile, but her zest, which had pulsated through me for decades, radiated.

"Mom, I have it all. And I've never thought about it till now, but I got that idea from you: You can have it all. You made your life work, even when the road you were on was not your choice. Getting married so young could have knocked you out, but you didn't get knocked out or knocked down. You just kept going. President of the garden club, organizing marches with Women Strike for Peace, and going back to school—who graduates from college at sixty-three? You!

"You had it all, and guess what? So do I! I have a great career, Ma. And you were my cheerleader. After I wrote my first book, you told me to get a publicist. I remember your words: 'Your father would be proud of you! He should have lived to see you now.'"

I kept going. I could not stop. I had to say it all. "I remember you telling me, 'If your father were alive, he'd say, "You gotta spend money to make money."'" I was surprised that I remembered so much about what she had done right. Even though she didn't tell me I was getting my tonsils out and deceived me with a story about my cousin's birthday party, I still loved her. And even though she had horrible judgment in telling me, just days after my father died, about the affair she'd had for eight years, I still loved her.

As I sat with her at this very moment, what registered on the front burner of my mind was that she did in fact support me, encourage me, and want more for me than she had. I felt her love and wanted to savor this precious feeling.

———

I was still there, at my mother's bedside, watching the moon rise. Larry had taken off his tie and his herringbone tweed sport jacket. His shirt looked wrinkled and worn out, which was how I imagined he was feeling and exactly how I was feeling. He was sitting on the couch, reading last week's *New York Times* Book Review section. He looked up and smiled at me. He said nothing, but his eyes said it all. I soaked in his concern, his love.

"What do you think about our planning to leave soon?" he asked.

I shook my head. I couldn't leave. "I'm not ready yet." I had more to say to my mother. "I think it's your time to let go, Ma." As soon as the words were out of my mouth, I wanted to take them back. I sounded harsh. I feared I *was* harsh, and selfish and self-centered. Now I knew that sometimes I was all the things I accused her of being.

I remembered a telephone call from Penny, a few years earlier.

"Judy, I have to make a suggestion. I hope it's okay with you." Penny's voice was softer than usual. She sounded a bit timid. What could be up?

"A suggestion?"

"I think your mom is overdue for an appointment with Dr. Scheinman. Did you ever call him?"

Who is Dr. Scheinman?

Penny explained. When she took my mother to have her pacemaker checked, Dr. Scheinman told her to remind me to make an annual appointment to check the batteries. "Those batteries don't last forever," Penny reminded me.

I felt like hanging up on her. My mother's pacemaker was inserted shortly after her Parkinson's diagnosis; how unaware my brother and I were then that the disease often led to long-term dementia. *What if the battery wasn't replaced?* Just remembering that moment evoked a sense of shame, but I knew juggling my feelings of responsibility and devotion with wanting to be free was common—and a heavy burden for care-givers. I had been obsessed with reading about the conflicted feelings of caregiving and end-of-life issues, and my reading had normalized my feelings.

Certainly, I was weary of managing my feelings of respon-sibility and devotion, balancing this heavy burden with my longing to be free of my mother. I was exhausted from juggling my terror of her leaving and my eagerness for her to go.

Seven o'clock, 7:05, 7:45, 8:05, 8:55. Time dragged on, and darkness settled in. The picture window on the other side of my mother's bed beckoned me. My reflection shimmered as I crossed the room to lean on the windowsill. Gazing into the outside world, I pressed my nose and forehead against the cold windowpane and peered into the night, alive with lights, traffic crawling on the distant highway just visible. A low-flying airplane flashed by, illuminating a grove of leafless maple trees swaying in the wind. A gust shook the branches, and a few remaining leaves fluttered down. I shut my eyes and remembered: I was huddled in the window seat, shivering and crying, nose against the glass of the small Allegheny Airlines plane awaiting takeoff on the JFK runway, en route to Burlington.

Burlington, Vermont, 1966

Wednesday, January 5, 1966. I sat next to my mother on the plane, sobbing.

"You're going to be okay, honey." My mother reached over to hold my hand, placing our two hands on my lap. I knew she wanted to be comforting, but I could not be comforted, and I was not okay, and I was certain I would never go back to being okay, because a voice was replaying it all in my mind, telling me, *"Are you sitting down? Please sit down."*

I could not stop revisiting the scene. The moment, from only two days earlier, was frozen in my mind. I had just opened the door of my apartment, rushed inside, thrown myself on my bed, and grabbed my still-ringing phone.

"Judy?"

"Michael?"

"It's Steve." *Why Steve? Why is Michael's roommate calling me?*

"Oh, Steve, sorry I missed you in Burlington, but Michael and I decided to ring in the new year at Times Square, so we drove down to New York on Friday."

"Judy, are you sitting down?"

"I just rushed in—why are you calling, Steve?"

"Are you sitting down?"

"I'm lying on my bed."

Steve paused. "I have bad news," he said, his voice trembling. "I don't know how to break it."

"Bad news?" *What could he be talking about?*

"Something . . . something's happened." His voice had dropped to a whisper.

"Happened?"

No response.

"Something's wrong?" I asked.

"Sit down, Judy. Sit down."

Why sit down?

"Michael?"

"Yes, Michael."

"Something's wrong?"

"Wrong. Yes, wrong."

Why isn't this making sense?

"Wrong? What?"

"There's been . . . an accident, Judy. The car. Jeff was driving . . ."

The sky was streaked with orange when Jeffrey showed up, late, on New Year's Day. Four in the afternoon was too late to start out from New York to Burlington, Michael had grumbled, and he wasn't much of a complainer.

"I love having the extra time for us," he'd said, "but we have a grueling drive ahead of us." The first year of medical school was more stressful than Michael had imagined it would be, and Monday was his longest clinic day. No way they'd be home before midnight. He'd start the week exhausted.

I agreed. Extra time to discuss wedding plans was delicious, but four o'clock was too late to start out on a long, slow drive in a classic MG with a canvas roof. Small car. Four p.m. Grueling drive. These little details felt insignificant at the time but later would replay on an endless loop.

I had met Michael at the University of Vermont in the steamy cafeteria line of the student union building two years before. He'd started a conversation with me about a book I was holding, and we had begun talking about literature: Anaïs Nin, Henry Miller, and E. E. Cummings.

Our connection had been immediate, triggered by the ephemeral chemistry that poets have been trying to quantify for years. Was it his thick, wavy, long blond hair I loved to run my fingers through or the intense, deep-blue eyes behind his delicate wire-rimmed eyeglasses that enchanted me? His wry sense of humor? His crooked smile? Tall and lanky, he had a dimple that appeared in his left cheek when he smiled or winked at me in unexpected moments. It was an attraction that deepened into something more as we began to know each other. We started out slowly, but soon, after an intense year together, we were solid and committed, newly engaged, and planning a May wedding.

We'd been skiing in Vermont for the holiday week but had decided to drive down to New York City to see the ball drop. His medical school friend Jeffrey, a lifelong pal from elementary school, was in Brooklyn and could give him a lift back to Burlington—how perfect. But once we'd arrived in New York, rather than go to Times Square, we opted to stay in my West End Avenue apartment, drinking champagne and making love.

———

"Take this," I insisted as we hugged by the green MG, saying goodbye. I wrapped my beige cashmere scarf around Michael's neck.

Michael had given it to me right after we got engaged. "It will keep you warm during the Burlington winters when I'm late at the hospital," he'd said. Our plan was to live in Burlington while he finished medical school.

It was bound to be drafty in that ridiculous car, which was cute but impractical. What I meant was, *If you can't take me with you, at least keep my scarf close and let my scent seep into your pores.*

Michael was tense about Jeff's lateness.

"Call me when you get home," I said, my fingers grasping his hair. "And it's only three weeks until I see you again."

"I'll call, hon, if it's not too late. Big hug for my girl."

"One last hug," I begged.

"Come on, you two!" Jeff called from the driver's seat. Defiantly, we nestled more deeply into each other, finally separating reluctantly. Shivering, I stood on the curb in front of my apartment building, waving until the shiny, dark green MG rounded the corner.

The orange streaks had disappeared.

———————————

"There was an accident," the voice over the phone said. "Judy, it was fatal. Instantaneous. They didn't have a chance."

It was fatal. Instantaneous. Every other word evaporated. Dangerous curve. Tractor-trailer. Blinding snow. Black ice. The two words echoed: *fatal, instantaneous.* That horrifying image wouldn't leave: a monstrous, eight-wheeled tractor-trailer colliding with the shiny, dark green convertible sports car with a canvas roof. Collided. Collision. Fatal. Instantaneous. Both dead, Michael and Jeff.

"Judy, Michael's funeral will be graveside, Wednesday," Steve said. "Up here in Burlington. I'm going to call you back later and tell you the details when I get them. I'll pick you up at the plane."

"Plane?"

"Airplane, Judy. Wednesday. You have to get a flight. Judy, who are you going to call now?"

Call now? Who will I call?

"Judy, I think you should call your mom. Do you know where she is? Please, call your mom. And call me back. Call your mom and call me back."

I don't remember calling, but I must have called her, because she and my father came, right away. They rushed to my apartment and found me lying on my bed, wrapped in the mauve satin quilt Michael and I had snuggled beneath two days earlier. My dad grabbed me, drew me close against his tweed sport jacket. His eyes were full. My mother lay down on my bed, hugging me tightly. My parents had pulled in living room chairs, and my father was sitting in one, close to the bed, hands on his knees, watching me closely. The four of us had sat together only weeks earlier, delighted to be planning our wedding.

I was still sobbing when the phone rang again. I picked it up.

"Is this Judy?"

It was Michael's mother, Lena. We'd been together just the week before, when Michael and I were up in Vermont. We'd been at Lena's on Christmas Day, which had coincided with the end of Hanukkah. It was the holiday gathering she orchestrated annually, complete with two dozen relatives, a Christmas tree, and menorah lighting ritual. Lena, dressed elegantly in a black velvet dress trimmed with lace and pearls, had been all smiles, proudly introducing me—her daughter-in-law-to-be—to family and friends. She had prepared a festive spread, a turkey dinner, complete with chestnut stuffing, candied sweet potatoes, a sautéed vegetable medley, and her dessert specialty: chocolate mousse pie sprinkled with candied rum sauce.

"Judy, don't come up here to the funeral, please," she said. In a shrill voice, she raged at me: had Michael not been in New York City, not needed a lift back to school with Jeffery, his reckless friend, the one with the MG; had they not left so late in the day because Jeffrey had to recuperate from a hangover; had there not been a whopping blizzard that left fresh snow piled on the road, fresh snow hiding the black ice; had there not been a monster tractor-trailer; had I not convinced her own Michael to drive down to New York for New Year's Eve (convinced or coerced, which was it?); had we not driven to New York—if not for all this, he would never have needed a lift, never gotten in the car with reckless Jeffrey. All this, Lena shrieked and sobbed. Had I not convinced or coerced him, Michael would be alive, right?

Oh my God, she *was* right. Driving my car down to New York *was* my idea. Had Michael not gotten a lift back to school with wild Jeffrey, his reckless friend with the tiny MG sportscar; had they not left so late in the day because Jeffrey had to recuperate from a hangover; had there not been a whopping blizzard that left fresh snow piled on the road, fresh snow hiding the black ice; had there not been a monster tractor-trailer . . .

"Stay away!" she screamed.

Numb and mute, I held the phone away from my ear.

"What?" my mother asked. "What's going on?"

"It's Michael's mother, Lena. She's blaming me! She says I should stay away. Not come to the funeral."

"Stay away? That's ridiculous. Give me the phone, Judy," my mother insisted. Her face was tight. "Hello, Lena. This is Peggy, Judy's mother. I am so sorry for your loss, and we are coming to the funeral," she said, before replacing the phone in its cradle.

Then my mother took my face in her hands and spoke to me in an unusually strong voice. "Of course you're going to the funeral, and I'll go with you." She pulled me close. "We'll go together. You belong there. This is not your fault, and you deserve to be at the funeral. This is his mother's worst nightmare; the poor woman is distraught. First she lost Michael's father when Michael was a baby, and now she has lost him. Poor woman. It's easier for her to blame you than to face what's happened and accept that bad things really do happen to good people. A really terrible thing has happened to her."

Nuzzling into her, I collapsed into her chest.

———

It was snowing lightly when our plane landed in Burlington that Wednesday, only five days after Michael and I had left and driven to New York City. Gray clouds hung, threatening. Steve met us at the airport, his eyes red and sunken. He looked as if he hadn't shaved in days. Michael's best friend, Burt, came, too, his clothes wrinkled and stained. Steve drove us to the cemetery and parked behind a long line of cars.

"Before we get out of the car, Judy," Steve said, "I want to tell you something. Keep away from Lena today. She's not herself. But Burt and I are here for you; we are with you."

"Let's avoid a scene," my mother said firmly. "Let's be sure not to sit near her." I nodded.

Steve took me by the arm, guiding and steadying me as we made our way through the cemetery, to the sole gravesite surrounded by mourners. The only sound was the crunch of our boots on the crusted snow. The sky was gray; the day cold and raw. The unearthed, dark soil was piled up, spotting the white snow. Steve and my mother held me up as we stood in the rear, amid the crowd. Numb and speechless, I listened to the familiar chant of the Mourner's Kaddish, the cadence and rhythm of the Hebrew words, heavy and timeless.

Yitgadal v'yitkadash sh'mei raba.
Oseh shalom bimromav, hu ya'aseh shalom,
Aleinu v'al kol-yisrael, v'imru:
Amen.

As the prayer finished, the wind picked up. Light snow began to fall. Lena and I exchanged neither a word nor a glance, not even when I stood at the edge of Michael's grave and tossed three shovelfuls of dirt onto his pine coffin. Shivering, I watched the snow flutter down while the casket containing my dreams sank into the frozen earth.

———

One month after the funeral, on a cold Tuesday night in February, the phone rang.

"Will you talk to me, Judy?" The voice was low, unfamiliar. I was silent, unsure who it was.

"Will you ever speak to me again?"

At first, I was numb; then it registered.

"Lena?"

"Yes, it's me." She spoke softly. "I'm sorry, sorry." Her voice cracked.

That spring, I flew up to Burlington, and she picked me up at the airport. We went to see Michael's grave together. I don't remember much, only that the sun was shining while we stood there, weeping. The cemetery was filled with wild daffodils swaying in the light breeze.

We stayed in touch for many years as we both tried to rebuild our lives. I believe she was happy for me when I married and began a family. Eventually, we drifted apart.

In 1993, I learned she had passed away at the age of 77.

Now, fifty years later, I rarely think of Michael. Except when it snows. Except when I see a mauve satin quilt like the one we huddled beneath. Except when I hear the name Michael. Except when I hear James Taylor's "How Sweet It Is (to Be Loved by You)." Except when I hear of a tragic accident on black ice. Except when I hear the Mourner's Kaddish in a synagogue or graveside.

I don't drive in snowstorms. I don't go to visit his grave. But every once in a while, when it's dusk and I step into the street, or if I'm about to get in my car when the sky has an orange glow, that dark Sunday afternoon lights up and explodes in my mind, and for a moment I find myself shivering, recalling what it was like to be lost and broken.

Now, when I think back to Michael's death, it is my mother I remember most vividly, lying next to me in my apartment, hugging me tightly as I weep on my bed, unable to absorb what I have lost. The sun is shining, but the shades are drawn and my room is dark and cold. I have the phone to my ear, and Lena is screaming, shrieking, sobbing, mourning her beautiful boy. *"Your fault, your fault"*—the words echo. My mother slowly takes the phone from my hands. She presses the receiver to her face. I cannot hear her words, but I see her speaking to Lena, and then she hangs up. She sits up on the bed, cradles my head in her lap, and kisses my forehead.

"Judy," she says, "we are going to Burlington for Michael's funeral. Together."

These words echo, too.

I feel my mother beside me on the plane. I feel her arm around me as we stand in the cemetery. The snow is falling as Michael's coffin is lowered into the ground, and I feel her pull me close, stopping me from collapsing into the snow. I nestle into the warmth of her fur coat.

It's these images of my mother—loving me, holding me, supporting me when the world around me had fallen apart—that are at the very heart of everything. For most of my life, I thought of her as a passive woman who followed orders from her mother, her husband, and the pediatrician. I saw her as an expert on cashmere sweaters and creating colorful Jell-O molds. But in that devastating moment, I saw her stand up—for me. What I saw and felt and sank into was her strength, her backbone. She would not allow Lena's blame to stop me. I had rarely seen her stand up for anyone, not even herself, not even when my father was unreasonable, critical, or even contemptuous. But in that excruciating moment when, devastated by grief, Lena lashed out at me, my mother saved me.

When "When" Is Now

Saturday, October 15: my birthday. Day three of the vigil that began with Jake's call on Thursday. I arrived early that morning.

"I'm back, Ma." I sat down in what was now "my chair." It was a little after nine in the morning. "Today's my birthday. We've been together sixty-nine years, Ma. More, if you count the nine months I lived in your belly."

My mother's eyes remained closed. Her body was still, unresponsive. *How long will she go on like this?* I wondered. I settled down, busily setting up and plugging in my laptop and cell phone, feeling worn out and exhausted

As the day wore on, family trickled in. Finally, after twenty-four hours of connecting flights, my brother, John, and his wife, Robin, arrived from Hawaii.

"It's your Johnny, Mom," he greeted her. My mom didn't budge, but I knew she absorbed his loving presence. By that afternoon, ten of us surrounded my mother's bed. Ilana, my brother's daughter, had brought a candle, and we filled my mother's small room with light and soft chanting. We were waiting.

Later that evening, I kissed her forehead when I left.

"Larry and I are going out with John and Robin for my birthday. I'm so sorry you can't come with us," I said. "We'll have a glass of wine for you, too, Ma. See you in the morning."

That night, we celebrated my birthday at a quaint French restaurant on Twenty-Third and Eighth. We were spent, and with not a lot new to say, the four of us finished two bottles of cabernet sauvignon, plus a bottle of champagne. Then the owner of the restaurant sent over some cognac. Finally, we closed the restaurant, made it to the street, and hailed a taxi. In the cab, we made our plan for the next day.

At five the next morning, the phone rang. "Your mother is gone," the nurse on duty said. "I'm so sorry."

I hung up and snuggled into my husband's arms. Then I called my brother.

We buried my ninety-three year old mother in a pine coffin. Rabbi Stephanie Ruskay, my niece, conducted her funeral. I remember the midmorning light illuminating the stained-glass windows and caressing Stephanie's face as she called us all up to the pulpit. My brother began by sharing a rich narrative that honored my mother's life. Then I recounted moments that attested to her vitality, her great spirit, and our enduring bond. (No, I didn't talk about my cousin Winnie's birthday party.) I described my mother as a woman of courage and grit. Her charm lived on in the stories told by my son and my husband, who both felt as if they were her number one grandson and number one son-in-law, respectively. A note of humor was injected into the ceremony when, from the first row in the sanctuary, my ex-husband, Arnie, got in on the act. He looked Larry straight in the eye and said, "She said you were number one? I thought *I* was the number one son-in-law."

Later that afternoon, we stood at the cemetery by the open grave adjacent to my father's tombstone. As I looked at the fresh soil piled up, waiting for my mother, I felt as if a volcanic pressure was beginning to lift.

PART EIGHT:

Retelling Our Stories

Create a ritual for yourself and your mother, whether it's lighting a candle, making a small altar of keepsakes, or writing something to or about her: a letter, a poem or just a few words. Be as creative as you like. Whether your mother is living or dead, the point is to honor the way she lives on inside you.

Revising and Revisiting

Our Stories

My mother left this earth the day after my sixty-ninth birthday. Eight years later, I am still retelling and revising my story.

For most of the final years of her life, my mother seemed to live in a timeless limbo, going in and out of a kind of wakeful oblivion. That's what Parkinson's and Lewy body dementia do. But somehow, at the very end, she seemed able to consciously orchestrate her final departure. She waited for my brother to return from Hawaii, giving them the opportunity to say goodbye to each other. By dying one day after my birthday, she spared my having to forever share the celebration of that occasion with the anniversary of her death.

A year after she died, on what would have been her ninety-fifth birthday, I dug out the Salvatore Ferragamo shoebox that had kept us company during the years of her slow decline. *Don't get maudlin*, I reminded myself, browsing through the photos. *She lived a long life, and her death was a blessing.* Eventually, I realized that perhaps what was making me tearful was that I had just celebrated an important milestone of my own: my seventieth birthday. My own aging, in the shadow of her death, was on my mind.

As I pored through the photos and memorabilia in the shoebox, I came across a photograph of a collage I'd made for my mother's eightieth birthday party. At the time, three years before her Parkinson's diagnosis, we had no idea how all of our lives were about to change.

As I examined the collage, one picture leaped out at me. It was a photograph of four of us: my mother; my six-year-old daughter, Rachel; my ten-year-old son, Zach; and me. My mother was wearing a traditional black graduation outfit. I smiled to think she would have called it an ensemble: a black robe and a square academic cap. A tassel from the square mortarboard cap that sat on her head swung with the breeze, and a huge smile covered her face. Sitting on my living room couch, gazing at that photo, I remembered the windy afternoon in May 1981 when we stood on the steps of Fordham University, celebrating a belated milestone in my sixty-three-year-old mother's life. Words from an exercise I'd led in numerous workshops surfaced:

> *Imagine you are looking at a photograph of your mother that has something important to tell you. Take your time and notice what you see: the shades, the shadows, the messages. Absorb all you can: the nuances, the backstory.*
>
> *Your mother is the most important woman you will ever know.*
>
> *Your mother welcomed you to womanhood.*

Judy, Daughter of Peggy: My Mother Graduated from Fordham at Sixty-Three

A year after my mother's second husband, Lenny, died, she called me with another surprise announcement. She was fifty-six years old and had lost two husbands, my father and Lenny, the lover whom she'd told me about shortly after my father's death. I was stunned when she told me she was thinking about going to college.

College? I had never heard her mention it. While my mother was not one to dwell on complaints, disappointments, or grief, unbeknownst to me, she must have harbored an inner yearning. Perhaps part of her had always mourned that she'd missed the rite of passage that college offered—leaving home and separating from her parents. Perhaps it was something else—living in an educated circle, she might have experienced deep shame about her less-than-proper education. Whatever she felt, there must have been a hidden spark.

A Jewish saying comes to mind: "Wherever there is a tiny spark, a great fire can be rekindled." Looking back, I wondered why my mother hadn't gone to college when she was younger, perhaps when my brother entered high school in the '60s, or later, during the empty-nest stage, when he and I were both gone. Perhaps she was insecure. Getting a college degree might have felt too daunting; she'd never been seen as an intellectual giant. On the contrary, my father had continually put her down as being "not so serious—or very bright." Perhaps she even feared upsetting my father by outdoing him. In their era, a wife with a college degree might have threatened my father's sense of identity. Perhaps her life was satisfying enough and she didn't want to risk unbalancing it. But in 1975, after losing two husbands, she felt something inside her shift. A tiny spark that must have been buried in the ashes was rekindled.

To my surprise, she'd done some investigation. She told me that Fordham University, where I was finishing my doctorate, was offering a new program aimed at supporting older adults returning to college. My mother needed to write up what she'd done with her life, and she might receive college credits for her "life experience." As it turned out, her life experience comprised many activities that my father had undervalued or even belittled. She would receive college credit for raising children; assisting my father's businesses by doing secretarial work and bookkeeping; and volunteering for the PTA, Brownies, Cub Scouts, garden club, and Women Strike for Peace. All this now had quantifiable worth and meaning.

To fulfill the admission requirements, my mother wrote up an autobiography. Three months after she submitted an application, she was accepted. I remember her pride upon learning she'd received one year of college credit—thirty credits—for all she had done.

"I saved a whole year of tuition," she said with a smile. "That's a couple of thousand dollars." Clearly, the process of writing about her life experience offered her a new lens through which to value and appreciate who she was and what she had done. What a gift.

Thus, as I was midway through finishing my doctorate, my mother began her undergraduate degree, both of us students at Fordham University, Lincoln Center, New York. Sometimes we'd meet for lunch in the cafeteria. At times she'd sit with my friends; at other times I'd sit with the friends she made. New friends, new beginnings.

As a student at Fordham, she spent the next five years plunging into new academic worlds of psychology, anthropology, sociology, and the history of religion and music. As she learned, her appetite and excitement grew. I was in awe of her enthusiasm for learning. By 1981, she had earned her bachelor of social work from my alma mater.

Ever since then, when I pause and reflect on what it actually took for my mother to return to college as a fifty-six-year-old, I feel my heart expand. It has occurred to me that I can't think of another person who has undertaken the challenge of returning to college after being out of high school for thirty-five years. How brave! As these thoughts emerged, I realized that my mother was a risk taker, yet it was unusual for me to think about her as brave or courageous. How had I missed this part of her story? How had I missed knowing her dreams? How had I missed acknowledging the strength and determination at her core?

I had always loved the red-boots story my mother used to tell about me when I was a little girl, how I'd been euphoric when she bought them for me and how she couldn't get them off me, and how the next morning she had looked outside and seen me on my red tricycle, naked, wearing nothing but the red boots. She always loved telling that story, so proud of my feistiness and high energy, proud of the way I broke the rules and danced to my own drummer.

Although I had not seen it for most of my life, she, too, had danced to the beat of her own drummer. And I had followed her! How had I been oblivious to the fact that my mother was the original girl in the red boots?

The Danger of a Single Story

Five years after my mother's death, I was prompted to rethink these questions when I came across a 2009 TED talk by Chimamanda Ngozi Adichie called "The Danger of a Single Story."

Chimamanda was born in Nigeria and came to the United States for college. When she arrived at Drexel University in Philadelphia, her roommate asked her where she had learned to speak English. Chimamanda had to tell her roommate that English is the official language of Nigeria. "Can you play some tribal music?" her roommate asked, and was surprised to learn that Chimamanda's favorite singer was Mariah Carey.

In 2009, Chimamanda delivered a talk that went viral. Her experience had taught her how she'd been limited by the story others held onto about Africa. All of us, she explained, rely on stories, which are actually stereotypes, to understand the complicated world we live in. It is not that stereotypes are untrue, but they are incomplete. They make one story become the only story.

For many years of my life, I held onto a single story. I saw my mother through the lens of my own disappointment as superficial and emotionally cut off. I harbored feelings of neglect and resentment. But as we both aged, and as I studied human nature as a psychotherapist and stopped expecting her to be like me, I began to see my mother differently. She rose to life as she suffered losses and challenges. I came to perceive her as a powerfully vital and resilient woman who was not afraid to go after what she wanted, whether it was a man who would meet her emotional needs or a college degree. She was exceptionally generous and incredibly proud of her children and of herself as a mother. The original girl with the red boots, she gave me permission to follow in her footsteps and to go beyond.

I believe I've been working on restoring my mother to her proper place for my whole life. In the many years I've written about and done workshops on the topic of mothers and daughters, I've known I was searching for my own healing.

In 1993, I wrote a chapter in a professional book about healing the mother-daughter relationship. I began this book with an epigraph from that chapter, a quote by Dr. Paula Caplan: "Although the expression of anger is both necessary and healing, what I have discovered is that it is not the inability to express anger that limits growth, but the inability to acknowledge and express love and caring." In writing this book, I have revised my narrative from a "Story of a Disappointed Daughter" to a "Story of a Grateful Daughter." My resentments have not evaporated but are now rebalanced with my sense of admiration for my imperfect mother. Grief has been my teacher, helping me understand, accept, and make peace with the fragility of life, the complexity of love, and the imperfections inherent in all relationships, especially mothering. I hope I have inspired you to examine your own story, too.

There's a line in Faulkner's novel *Requiem for a Nun* that I love: "The past is never dead. It's not even past." The truth is, we don't know when we might unexpectedly shake up a forgotten story. Just like the shifting images in the sand-art picture in my office, our understanding of our own story is always deepening and evolving, remaining open to change and transformation.

Appendix:
Guided Imageries

The active imagination/guided-imagery exercises introducing each chapter and scattered throughout the book are included here and can serve as prompts for your own inner work. We never know when we might shake up a forgotten story: feel free to contact me with any unexpected surprises or mysteries at drjudithrabinorphd@gmail.com.

Part One: Welcome to Womanhood
Imagine that you are searching through a box of old photographs, seeking a picture of your mother. Find one that strikes you, and look at it closely. Notice the expression on your mother's face. What is she wearing? Notice her clothing. What is the background of this picture? If it is outdoors, what is the weather like? The light? If it is indoors, what furnishings do you see? If there are other people in the picture, how is she relating to them? As you contemplate her at this particular moment in her life, be aware of what she is feeling.

Part Two: The Secret
Close your eyes and think about a secret that was kept from you. Breathe deeply. Who kept the secret from you? How

did you feel when the secret was revealed? If nothing comes to mind, perhaps a secret you hold has emerged. Think about a secret you keep or maybe have kept. Focus on the feelings that come up. Where does your body feel that secret? What is the sensation it causes in your muscles? What feelings and associations arise?

Part Three: Becoming a Therapist

We all carry pain. Our muscles hold on to feelings and memories. Can you locate emotional pain or energy in particular areas of your body? Sadness? Anger? Hunger for connection? Breathe deeply into any of your hurt places. Inhale deeply, exhale completely. Nothing to do, nowhere to go—just notice what happens in your body when you breathe into the places where emotions gather. Does the breath soften you? Or do your muscles tighten as you breathe? How does being with pain impact your body?

Part Four: Love, Marriage, and Divorce

Imagine it is the holiday before you were born: Thanksgiving, New Year's Day, Christmas, Passover, or the Fourth of July. Imagine your mother sitting at the holiday table, pregnant with you. How does she feel about her pregnancy? Who is at the table with her? Who is missing? Take a moment to breathe into the image. Feel that primordial connection to her, that connection with her that defies language.

Part Five: Mother-Daughter Complications

Think about a story you have told repeatedly about your mother, whether it is about something humorous, tragic, or difficult, or a moment of happiness between you. Imagine telling it again, to someone who is listening attentively. Notice how you feel in your body as you tell this story. What does this story tell you about the mother who raised you? Why do you like to tell it?

268 The Girl in the Red Boots

Part Six: Making Peace

Imagine your mother alone in a reflective moment. Maybe she stops in the middle of a daily activity, like paying bills or washing dishes, and just gazes into the middle distance or out the window. She is unaware you are watching her. What observations do you make of her in such a moment? What do you imagine preoccupies her? Is she daydreaming? What is on her mind?

Part Seven: When "When" Is Now

Imagine that your mother is standing in the doorway of a room you are seated in. See her searching. She is looking for you, and when she finds you, she wants to come in and sit by you. How do you feel in your body as your mother spots you? Have you made eye contact? If so, what's that like? Check in with yourself. Do you look at her with a welcoming gaze, or do you turn away? How do you feel about her coming into the room and sitting beside you?

Part Eight: Retelling Our Stories

Create a ritual for yourself and your mother, whether it's lighting a candle, making a small altar of keepsakes, or writing something to or about her: a letter, a poem, or just a few words. Be as creative as you like. Whether your mother is living or dead, the point is to honor the way she lives on inside you.

> * Imagine that you are looking at a photograph of your mother that has something important to tell you. Take your time and notice what you see: the shades, the shadows, the messages. Absorb all you can: the nuances, the backstory.
>
> Your mother is the most important woman you will ever know.
>
> Your mother welcomed you to womanhood.

* Note: see page 258.

Acknowledgments

The seeds for this book were planted twenty-five years ago, when my daughter, Rachel, left for college and I joined a writing group. I have written it in bits and pieces over these many years, and it has undergone numerous transformations. Along the way, many people have supported me, reading different versions and generously offering insights and comments. The book was especially enriched by the contributions of Didi Goldenhar, Karen Propp, my Wednesday consultation group, and my Tuesday-night writing group (formerly Charles Salzman's writing class) at the The Marlene Meyerson JCC Manhattan.

Many dear friends, colleagues, and relatives—too numerous to list here—have read various renditions. To name a few, I thank Liz Burk, Nancy Bravman, Judith Brisman, Judi Goldstein, Sheila Rindler, and Jane Stein for their time, energy, and support.

Two people who helped me see my deeper story deserve special mention. Laura Zinn Fromm supported me in deepening my perspective. Later, Regina McBride helped me give birth to the arc that shapes this book and changed my understanding of my life.

Special thanks to Brooke Warner, Lauren Wise, Annie Tucker, and the staff at She Writes Press.

Without my patients, this book would not exist. Deep gratitude.

Gratitude to Arnold Rabinor, ex-husband and father of my precious children, who supported my dream to become a psychologist. May his memory be a blessing. Endless thanks to my children, Rachel and Zachary, for a lifetime of love, thoughtful conversations and more. Larry Wetzler, my husband, has been behind me throughout as a loving supporter and a rigorous critic. His consistent love, interest, artistic sensibility, and patient encouragement have given me the strength to keep writing even when I doubted I had something worth saying.

About the Author

Judith Ruskay Rabinor, PhD, is a psychologist, clinician, author, writing coach, speaker, and workshop leader. In addition to her New York City private psychotherapy practice, she offers remote consultations for writers, clinicians, and families. She has written dozens of articles for both the public and professionals and has published two books, *A Starving Madness: Tales of Hunger, Hope and Healing* (Gurze Books, 2002) and *Befriending Your Ex After Divorce: Making Life Better for You, Your Kids and Yes, Your Ex!* (New Harbinger Publications, 2012). A sought-after speaker and workshop leader, Judy speaks at national and international mental health conferences and runs workshops at spas, universities, and retreat centers.

Reach Judy at www.judithruskayrabinorphd.com

Author photo © Judith Ruskay Rabinor, PhD

SELECTED TITLES FROM SHE WRITES PRESS

She Writes Press is an independent publishing company founded to serve women writers everywhere. Visit us at www.shewrites press.com.

Motherlines: Letters of Love, Longing, and Liberation by Patricia Reis. $16.95, 978-1-63152-121-8. In her midlife search for meaning, and longing for maternal connection, Patricia Reis encounters uncommon women who inspire her journey and discovers an unlikely confidante in her aunt, a free-spirited Franciscan nun.

The Shelf Life of Ashes: A Memoir by Hollis Giammatteo. $16.95, 978-1-63152-047-1. Confronted by an importuning mother 3,000 miles away who thinks her end is nigh—and feeling ambushed by her impending middle age—Giammatteo determines to find The Map of Aging Well, a decision that leads her on an often-comic journey.

I'm the One Who Got Away: A Memoir by Andrea Jarrell. $16.95, 978-1-63152-260-4. When Andrea Jarrell was a girl, her mother often told her of their escape from Jarrell's dangerous, cunning father as if it was a bedtime story. Here, Jarrell reveals the complicated legacy she inherited from her mother—and shares a life-affirming story of having the courage to become both safe enough and vulnerable enough to love and be loved.

Her Beautiful Brain: A Memoir by Ann Hedreen. $16.95, 978-1-938314-92-6. The heartbreaking story of a daughter's experiences as her beautiful, brainy mother begins to lose her mind to an unforgiving disease: Alzheimer's.

Don't Leave Yet: How My Mother's Alzheimer's Opened My Heart by Constance Hanstedt. $16.95, 978-1-63152-952-8. The chronicle of Hanstedt's journey toward independence, self-assurance, and connectedness as she cares for her mother, who is rapidly losing her own identity to the early stages of Alzheimer's.